Dominique's

Dominique's

Dominique D'Ermo

E. P. DUTTON · NEW YORK

Published in the United States by E. P. Dutton,
a division of NAL Penguin Inc.,
2 Park Avenue, New York, N.Y. 10016.

Published simultaneously in Canada
by Fitzhenry and Whiteside, Limited, Toronto.

Library of Congress Cataloging-in-Publication Data

D'Ermo, Dominique, 1927–
Dominique's.
Includes index.
1. Cookery. 2. Dominique's (Restaurant:
Washington, D.C.) I. Title.
TX715.D46   1987   641.509753   87-13659
ISBN: 0-525-24580-4

COBE

Designed by Mark O'Connor

10 9 8 7 6 5 4 3 2 1

First Edition

To my niece Lindsay D'Ermo-Owens

Contents

Acknowledgments

The huge success of Dominique's Restaurants testifies to the professionalism of our employees and the faithfulness of our customers.

My grateful thanks to our chefs, our cooks, and the mosaic of customers who come from all walks of life and from all over the world.

Thanks to Diana Damewood, my manager, who gave me the freedom to work on this book by releasing me from my administrative duty at the Washington, D.C., restaurant.

Many people were involved in the making of this book, including Chef Pascal Oudin and his assistants, Erich and Pablo, and Adolfo Olivera, our chef from our Washington operation with his dedicated kitchen staff.

Thanks go to Marta Lorenz-Talleyrand from the Alexander Hotel in Miami Beach, who corrected, tested, and edited many of our recipes.

Grateful thanks to Valerie Hart, who has always inspired me with her friendship and beautiful food creations.

Acknowledgments

An added thanks for all my friends who have contributed some of their favorite recipes to this book.

And last but not least, my editor, Susan Knopf, a very talented lady whose English is better than mine.

Foreword

In 1974 Dominique D'Ermo opened his restaurant in Washington, on Pennsylvania Avenue, just three blocks from the White House. With its good food, good wine list, and charming environment, it was successful almost immediately, beginning to compete with the big names in Washington—French food, where-can-we-be-seen restaurants. In those days, Democrats tended to eat in one place and Republicans in another. But soon, as Dominique was to learn—and the late eighties proved—Democrats and Republicans alike came and went, but good food and good restaurants, and good hosts are eternal . . . almost.

In 1976, a long article appeared in the Portfolio section of The Washington Star, which was to make this immortality possible, or at least possible sooner. Willie Morris, the distinguished author and journalist wrote, on Sunday, February 29, a loving and inviting paean to his newly discovered favorite spot in the nation's capital. It put Dominique's on the map. Later, Dominique's reputation would spread, earning him international awards, four stars, and many other tributes, and impelling him to open a sister restaurant in Miami Beach. The rest is gourmet history, but it started with Willie Morris's wonderful piece, reprinted here with his kind permission.

I've Found My La Belle Aurore

Do you remember La Belle Aurore in *Casablanca,* where Bogart and Bergman used to hang out and drink champagne and listen to Sam play the song, back in those fine days before the Germans came to Paris? The world always welcomed lovers then, until the Nazis arrived to muck it up, and Bergman left Bogart standing in the rain at the Gare du Nord.

I've found my La Belle Aurore, which by circumstance is just down Pennsylvania Avenue from the White House, a joyous little place with Impressionists on the walls and food and wine good enough to bring your favorite girl and say to her, "Here's looking at you, kid," or if you're in a mood of introspection to tell her you've been around long enough to know that the problems of three people don't amount to a hill of beans in this crazy world.

It's called Dominique's, and it's also fitting that Dominique D'Ermo, a generous and buoyant owner, was in the French Resistance when he was a boy and says that if a German in one of those green uniforms which haunt him from his boyhood came in the door, he would tell him the place was sold out. He left France after the war because he was tired of all the Frenchmen fighting each other for the "grandeur of France."

One of the clichés about Washington is that people go to restaurants to be seen, much as people do in Manhattan when they go to "21" or Elaine's or the old Sardi's, but my friend Dominique says that the same people who go to those places to look and be looked at come to his place just to enjoy themselves. He has sat down at my table of an evening with a bottle of Dom Perignon and told me the story of his life, which in some ways is a peculiarly indigenous Washington story even if it doesn't seem so on the surfaces, and I think if we heard the rumble of big guns from twenty miles away as they did in La Belle Aurore that day in 1940, Dominique would get word to the Germans, or the Russkies, as Bogart warned the Gestapo major concerning New York, that they would take certain sections of this town at their own risk.

Dominique gets a lot of lawyers, doctors, politicians, bankers, OAS and State Department people, secretaries and their bosses. One night recently Mr. Levi, the attorney general, and Mr. Justice Powell were in earnest conversation at a table. A big shot from the State Department comes in three nights a week, with different girls each time, and Dominique says all three are in love with the man. He bought his restaurant about a year ago when it was called Jacqueline's, and then it was known as a place where State Department people always brought their mistresses. Romances are made here at lunch, he says, and broken at dinner. A couple came in for lunch a couple of days ago and were very cozy and happy, and they came back for dinner and got in an awful fight. A man named Martin made a late-night reservation and came in on time with a lady. "Mr. Martin?" Dominique asked, and the man said yes, then "Mrs. Martin?" and the lady said, "I'm not Mrs. Martin, I'm Mrs. Johnson," and Dominique said, "Right this way, Mrs. Johnson."

He came to Washington in 1962. He had attained, he says, the zenith of the pastry business, and had written the bible of all the pastry chefs in America, *The Pastry Chef's Guide to Modern Baking.* After that he became an executive with the Shoreham Hotel in Washington, D.C., and the Princess Hotels International. Before he took out his American citizenship papers in 1956 he worked in some of the best spots in Europe, including the Savoy and the Dorchester in London. He worked for a while in Miami Beach, where he got in with a crowd of mad French gamblers who played the horses and dogs in the afternoons and shot craps by night, but the only things the patrons of the hotel where he worked wanted were apple pie and cheesecake. Sometimes they wanted swans and elephants made out of ice cream or crushed ice. This was a letdown for him after the Savoy, and that was when he decided he wanted his own restaurant someday.

Dominique knows a great deal about life, all its swirls and dervishes, and that includes the French community in Washington. When he talks about them, and about his days in France during the Occupation, his accent is a little like Chevalier's and you have to lean down over the champagne glass to listen more closely, or else you will lose the nuances. "Let me tell you about the French colony here. Most of the French in Washington outside of the Embassy are hairdressers, waiters, kitchen employees, restaurateurs. The French people like to be organized.

It's the only similarity they have with the Germans. The French must have someone to tell them what to do. Since nobody's telling them what to do here, the French community you have here is very chaotic."

He was standing on a street corner on the Champs-Élysées one afternoon in November after the war. "I'd just come back from all the blood and scenes of horror with the Resistance and the war, I heard guns and screams." All around him Frenchmen were beating each other up. The veterans of Free France were once again clashing with the Communists. A man came toward him and punched him with a pair of brass knuckles. He was in the hospital ten days, and when he got out he told his family and friends, "I can't stay here anymore." And to London he went.

He was a teenage boy in the Occupation, living in the woods around Lyons. He and his friends distributed underground newspapers, stole buses and trucks for their transportation, and robbed drugstores for cigarettes to give to the Resistance fighters; and then he got in much deeper with them. In 1943 the instructions from the Liberation were to liberate two cities: Nantua and Oyonnax in the region of Savoie. They ran up the Cross of Lorraine in these places and at least for a while were the heroes of France. These were the only two cities occupied by the Free French during the war. Not long after, the Germans brought a whole Panzer division into southern France. While you're on your way there, they were told, you might just as well destroy the Resistance occupying those towns. "They came in quickly with many planes, tanks, and troops; they had the help of the French collaborators, and let me tell you there was no pity. We had bazookas, stun guns, and grenades, and that was as far as we went.

"We were scared because we were so young. All of us were between sixteen and twenty-two years old. I was in a truck on a road trying to escape when one of those Messerschmidt 110s dove down. I saw the German pilot, I saw the flame coming out of the guns. I was hypnotized. I thought of my aunt, who'd died in a monastery and told me we'd meet someday in paradise. The truck was destroyed—I couldn't move. My friends were in a ditch shouting, 'Dominique, Dominique. Jump! Jump!' I thought, if I move my blood will run out of my guts. Then we ran away from the Germans. We ran and ran and starved to death. We begged bread and butter from people who gave it to us and then told us to leave." Five days later, they arrived at a railroad track about three miles from Nantua and saw eight or ten German soldiers. They had a conference among themselves about whether they should starve to death, or surrender, or be killed. "We were tired, beat, hungry, and we gave up."

They were taken to Gestapo headquarters. Fifty people were put in a cell half the size of his restaurant. They were interrogated two or three times a day about where they had gotten their bread and guns. Later they were taken to the court-house in Nantua, ten of them chained together. "The same people who greeted us a week before were spitting on us, jeering at us. I was crying so much, I was so afraid. They didn't kill us. They kept us in jail. I remember those terrible days, sitting here in my restaurant three blocks from the White House, entertaining senators and diplomats. How strange it seems now. We could've been transported to the hills or killed." The Germans and the French collaborators shot more than five hundred young patriots in a two-week period.

Dominique sits now at his favorite table, orders some more champagne. The waiters bustle by with the fine camaraderie of the place. People know each other here, and send over greetings to him and to other tables. Dominique and I are still talking about the war, about suffering, and about America. "The Germans were murderers by profession. The members of the Resistance became murderers to defend our country. Germans killing French. French killing each other. You get people to die, people to suffer, people to survive, and that's what it's all about."

And then he laughs a little. "From all the blood and tears, I even feel relaxed now. Relaxed and happy. . . . I own my own little business and it's three blocks from the White House. I walk around a lot. This afternoon was a beautiful day. While I was walking I met about ten people I knew—lawyers, people in government, businessmen, and office workers who are all customers of Dominique, and they all said hello to me with a smile. From all the chaos and blood of that time I thought: I really am proud of this civilization. It's a great feeling, just to have this freedom here. I'm Dominique D'Ermo, nobody's going to tell me what to do. I'm an American. This is a refuge from the barbarians, because Western civilization is protected here. And the people will die for it if they have to."

And then he adds: "And on top of that, my friend, I'm interested in what's on your plate and what's in your glass." At which point, if one is the romantic I am, you would expect to hear a little something from the original score, the brass and violins, slipping from "La Marseillaise" into Sam's piano, the love songs and laughter, the hearts full of passion, the jealousy and hate.

—WILLIE MORRIS

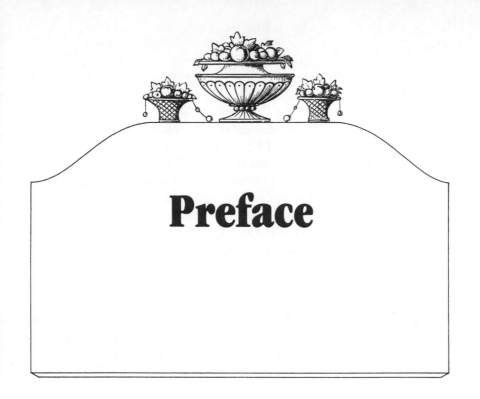

Preface

Being born and raised in France gave me the opportunity to taste the finest in food. At a very young age I learned to admire and respect the great chefs of the world for their hard work, perseverance, and endless imagination.

After working in some of the finest restaurants in Europe, coming to America and moving up to become an executive in the industry, I felt the time was right for me to open my own restaurant—Dominique's Famous French Restaurant in Washington, D.C.

In those days you could read the menus of most French restaurants and see the same items being served time after time. I knew it would take a special touch to make Dominique's different from my competition. I had acquired many exotic game, fish, and meat recipes during my travels and professional experience, and I decided to add these to the more sophisticated continental cuisine of my menu.

The idea worked so well that it began to mold even the ambience of the restaurant. We added stuffed rattlesnakes, birds, and animal heads on the walls of one of the dining rooms and enhanced the elegance of candlelight with etched and stained-glass partitions.

When I was shopping the country for a second location, I could have chosen from a dozen sophisticated dining-out cities along the Atlantic or Pacific coasts. Instead, I picked Miami Beach—a sultry city that, until recently, had trouble shaking its reputation as a crumbling retirement home and winter sanctuary for grumbling New Yorkers. The glitz and glitter evoked by entertainments such as television's "Miami Vice" brilliantly reflect a reborn city tuned to creativity in the kitchen and dazzle in the dining room. For this southern operation I chose to set up shop at the elegant Alexander All-Suite Hotel, a luxurious beach-front hotel frequented by the kind of guests who know good food and are accustomed to dining at my sort of restaurant.

I was fortunate in both my restaurants to have talented chefs, such as Adolfo Olivera and Pascal Oudin, able to read my mind and then to create their own recipes and presentations. It is a pleasure to watch Adolfo, Pascal, and their staffs, because the harder they work, the bigger their smiles. We are constantly learning, and therefore our menus are constantly changing.

This book takes for granted that you know a little bit about cooking, and these recipes are here to complement what you already know. I have included recipes that are simple and quick, as well as those that are more complicated and require more work and longer preparation. These recipes represent the best from both of my menus. Some recipes that can be found in every cookbook I have not included, though they may sometimes be on one of our menus. The truth is, even the more common dishes like Caesar salad are very special creations at Dominique's.

When preparing any dish, it is important to remember to buy only the freshest ingredients. Here in America we have an endless variety of fresh vegetables, meats, and fish. The texture, flavor, and ultimately the quality of any dish depends primarily on the raw ingredients. I am constantly bringing in fresh food from all over the world—fresh trout from West Virginia, fresh frogs' legs from France or southern Florida, fresh salmon from Norway, fresh stone crabs from Florida, fresh berries from Australia, fresh mussels from Maine, and even fresh rattlesnake meat from Arizona or Texas.

In addition to our fish, we purchase our meat and vegetables only from the best purveyors in town with very high specifications for top quality and freshness—because without this concern, I feel we will not last. Quality will always prevail.

At both our restaurants, we use fresh herbs, and you should also try to do so in these recipes. If fresh herbs are not available and the recipe does not give an amount for dried herbs, use one-quarter of the amount of fresh herb listed. Also remember to replace the dried herbs in your kitchen regularly, since they do lose their flavor.

I must thank a talented and dedicated staff for helping to give Dominique's restaurants the quality of excellence in service and cuisine—Diana Damewood, my dining room manager, being the star of all stars. Thanks to all my intelligent kitchen staff, and especially to Pablo and Erich in our Miami Beach operation and Frank and Ype in our Washington restaurant.

I and my chefs are only as good as the people behind us. We are fortunate to be working with the best. Enjoy!

—DOMINIQUE D'ERMO

Appetizers and Pasta

First courses range from tasty spreads on toasted bread to an elegant plate of Lobster Ravioli. If you are planning a large gathering or cocktail party, choose a simple recipe that will feed a number of people, such as Caviar Mousse or one of the terrines. If you want a more formal first course, try the Bavaroise of Smoked Fish with Tomato Vinaigrette, or Linguine with Wild Mushrooms. Many of the recipes in this chapter, especially the pasta dishes, can be served as light meals for lunch or dinner, accompanied by a salad, some French bread, and a good bottle of wine.

Artichokes with Caviar

SERVES 4

4 medium artichokes
8 ounces caviar (best quality you can afford)
1 1/3 cups sour cream
4 lemon wedges for garnish

Trim the artichokes and cook in boiling salted water, uncovered, for about 35 minutes, or until tender. Remove from the pot and invert on paper towels to drain. With a spoon, remove the hairy choke from the center, and place the artichokes in the refrigerator to chill. The artichokes can be prepared ahead up to this point, covered, and refrigerated until ready to use.

Just before serving, combine the caviar with the sour cream. Spoon a quarter of this mixture into the center of each artichoke, and serve with lemon wedges.

Mushrooms Stuffed with Seafood

SERVES 4

12 large mushroom caps, cleaned
6 tablespoons butter, melted
4 shallots, finely minced
⅓ cup bread crumbs
2 tablespoons chopped fresh parsley
6 shrimp, peeled and finely chopped, or 6 oysters, shucked and finely
  chopped
3 tablespoons dry white wine
1 teaspoon chopped fresh tarragon, or ¼ teaspoon dried
1 egg yolk, lightly beaten
3 tablespoons heavy cream
Salt and freshly ground pepper to taste
4 tablespoons grated Parmesan
Paprika

Preheat the oven to 400°F.

Remove the stems from the mushrooms, leave the caps whole, and set aside. Chop the stems finely, and sauté in 2 tablespoons melted butter with the shallots, until the stems and shallots are tender. Add the bread crumbs, parsley, shrimp or oysters, wine, and tarragon and bring to a boil. Remove from the heat.

In a small bowl, beat together the egg yolk and cream with

a wire whisk. Stir into the sautéed mixture, blending well. Season with salt and pepper. Fill the mushroom caps with the stuffing mixture, rounding it high. Brush with the remaining melted butter, sprinkle with Parmesan and paprika, and bake 10 minutes.

Peppers and Anchovies Ratatouille

SERVES 4

We serve this as a vegetable garniture for chicken and veal in the restaurants, but it's also delicious spread on crackers or bread as an appetizer.

2 tablespoons olive oil
2 pounds peppers (approximately 5 to 6), green and red mixed, cut into
*   1/2-inch julienne strips*
2 tablespoons capers, drained
3 garlic cloves, minced
1 tablespoon fresh oregano, or 1/2 teaspoon dried
2 tablespoons tomato paste
2 tablespoons red wine vinegar
1 1/2 cups peeled, seeded, and diced tomatoes
One 2-ounce can anchovies (see Note)
2 tablespoons chopped fresh parsley
12 black Greek olives, pitted
Salt and freshly ground pepper to taste

Heat the oil in a large skillet. Add the pepper strips and cook over high heat, stirring from time to time. Add the capers, garlic, and oregano and stir to combine.

　　While the pepper mixture cooks, mix the tomato paste and the vinegar in a small bowl and blend in the chopped tomatoes.

3

Add this to the peppers and mix thoroughly. Cover and simmer slowly, until the peppers are soft but still crunchy, about 10 minutes.

Remove the anchovies from the oil, drain carefully, rinse with cold water, and chop coarsely. When the peppers are done, remove from the heat and immediately stir in the anchovies. Cover and set aside.

To serve cold, refrigerate. To serve hot, proceed with the recipe. Just before serving, stir in the parsley and olives and season with salt and pepper.

NOTE: It is most important that the quality of canned anchovies is the very best you can buy. I suggest anchovies canned in oil. It is also important to remove the excess salt from the anchovies, or you will spoil the dish.

Bavaroise of Smoked Fish with Tomato Vinaigrette

SERVES 4

This elegant first course, made the night before, is well worth the effort. It also makes a nice light luncheon or brunch dish for special occasions.

BAVAROISE

8 ounces sturgeon, cut into 1-inch pieces
1/2 teaspoon salt
1/2 teaspoon freshly ground pepper
Juice of 1/2 lemon
8 ounces smoked salmon, cut into 1-inch pieces
2 cups heavy cream
12 thin slices smoked salmon
4 ounces black caviar (best quality you can afford)

TOMATO VINAIGRETTE

1 large, ripe tomato, peeled, seeded, and diced
1 tablespoon tomato paste
6 tablespoons sherry wine vinegar
2 tablespoons chopped fresh basil
½ cup olive oil
1 cup tomato juice
Salt and freshly ground pepper to taste

Prepare the bavaroise the night before. In a food processor fitted with the steel blade or in a food mill, purée the sturgeon, sieve into a medium bowl, and season with half the salt, pepper, and lemon juice; cover and refrigerate. Clean the processor or food mill, then prepare the smoked salmon pieces in the same manner. Fold half the heavy cream into the sturgeon purée and half into the salmon purée.

Line the bottom and sides of 4 individual ½-cup soufflé molds with the smoked salmon slices, using 3 slices for each mold. Spread one-fourth of the sturgeon purée in the bottom of each lined mold, sprinkle with one-fourth of the caviar, and cover with one-fourth of the salmon purée. Cover and chill overnight.

To prepare the Tomato Vinaigrette, purée the tomato, tomato paste, vinegar, and basil in a food processor or blender until smooth. Whir in the olive oil and tomato juice, season with salt and pepper, and refrigerate until ready to use.

To assemble, coat 4 plates with the Tomato Vinaigrette, unmold the bavaroise on top, and serve cold.

Caviar Mousse

SERVES 18

This is a cocktail party favorite and very simple to prepare.

4 ounces red caviar (best quality you can afford)
4 ounces black caviar (best quality you can afford)
2 tablespoons chopped fresh tarragon
2 tablespoons minced onion
1 teaspoon grated lemon peel
2 cups sour cream
1 envelope unflavored gelatin, softened in 1/4 cup cold water
1 cup heavy cream, whipped
6 large spinach leaves, rinsed well and patted dry
Sour cream for garnish
Chopped fresh chives for garnish
Pumpernickel or rye bread, sliced

Combine the red and black caviar. Add the tarragon, onion, and lemon peel, then fold in 2 cups sour cream. Add the gelatin and blend well. Gently fold in the whipped cream. Pour the caviar mixture into a lightly oiled 1-quart soufflé mold. Chill in the refrigerator, covered, for about 5 hours.

To serve, unmold on a serving platter lined with spinach leaves, garnish with sour cream and chives, and surround with bread slices.

Curried Crab
in Tiny Cream Puffs

SERVES 8 TO 12

Crab and curry, with a reduction of shallots and cream, make an excellent blend. For an elegant cocktail nibble, we spoon this mixture into miniature cream puffs.

2 tablespoons unsalted butter
1/4 cup minced shallots
2 cups heavy cream
1/4 cup dry vermouth
1 1/2 teaspoons curry powder, or more for a hotter flavor
Salt and freshly ground pepper to taste
1/2 teaspoon fresh lemon juice
1 teaspoon Dijon mustard
3/4 pound cleaned cooked crabmeat
24 tiny cream puffs (see following recipe), halved horizontally
Chutney or paprika for garnish

In a medium skillet over moderate heat, melt the butter and sauté the shallots until soft but not brown. Add the cream, bring to a boil, stir in vermouth, and over high heat, reduce the mixture to 1 cup. Add the curry powder, salt, pepper, lemon juice, and mustard. Taste, adjust the seasoning as necessary, and set aside to cool slightly.

When ready to serve, fold in the crabmeat, then spoon the mixture into the bottom halves of the cream puffs. Dot with chutney or dust with paprika, then put the tops of the cream puffs loosely in place, and serve at once.

Cream Puff Paste

MAKES 24 CREAM PUFFS

¾ cup water
6 tablespoons butter
1 generous pinch of salt
3 pinches of sugar
¾ cup all-purpose flour
3 medium eggs

Preheat the oven to 400°F.

Combine the water, butter, salt, and sugar in a deep pan and bring to a boil. Simmer until all the ingredients are melted. Remove from the heat and stir in the flour all at once. Beat rapidly with a wooden spoon until the mixture is a smooth paste. Return to low heat and stir rapidly until the mixture pulls away from the sides of the pan. Remove from the heat and add the eggs, 1 at a time, mixing well after each addition. The batter should be the same consistency as a thick cream, yet solid enough to hold its shape.

Drop the batter from a teaspoon onto a lightly greased baking sheet, for tiny puffs. Bake 10 minutes, or until the puffs have risen. Then lower the temperature to 350°F. and continue baking 15 minutes, or until done. If underbaked, the cream puffs will collapse while cooling. Cool on a rack.

NOTE: To speed up preparation of the Curried Crab at mealtime, the cream puffs may be baked a day ahead. Once baked thoroughly and cooled, refrigerate the puffs in a tightly covered container. The cream puffs may also be baked ahead and frozen. At serving time, place the frozen puffs in a preheated 400°F. oven for a few minutes to thaw, then proceed with the recipe.

Baked Oysters with Cheese

SERVES 4

2 tablespoons butter
2 tablespoons all-purpose flour
1 cup light cream
1 pinch of salt
1 pinch of white pepper
1 tablespoon finely chopped fresh dill, or ½ teaspoon dried
1 dash of ground nutmeg
16 oysters, shucked, bottom shells reserved
4 strips of bacon, cooked, drained, and crumbled
1 cup grated Cheddar or Monterey Jack cheese

Melt the butter in a small saucepan and add the flour, cooking for several minutes over low heat and stirring constantly. Remove from the heat and add the cream, salt, and pepper, stirring until smooth. Return the pan to medium heat and cook, stirring constantly, until thickened. Stir in the dill and nutmeg, and set aside.

Chop the oysters coarsely. Put 2 tablespoons of the reserved sauce into each of the 16 reserved shells, and fill with chopped oysters. Top with the crumbled bacon and grated cheese. Place in a preheated broiler, and broil for a few minutes, until the cheese melts.

Oysters Dominique

SERVES 2

All you need for this delicious appetizer is fresh oysters, a good garlicky tomato sauce, and freshly grated Parmesan.

12 oysters on the half shell
6 tablespoons Marinara Sauce (see following recipe)
3 tablespoons freshly grated Parmesan

Arrange the oysters on a bed of rock salt or on a cast-iron oyster platter. Spoon a little Marinara Sauce over each oyster, and sprinkle with Parmesan. Place under a preheated broiler for 5 to 6 minutes, or until the oysters are cooked.

Marinara Sauce

MAKES 2 QUARTS

This recipe makes a large quantity, but it freezes beautifully and will keep for 2 months or more. For easy use, freeze in small batches and defrost only what you need for the recipe.

1/3 cup olive oil
2 garlic cloves, finely chopped
2 cups finely chopped Spanish onions
4 cups peeled, seeded, and chopped ripe tomatoes, or one 28-ounce can
*   Italian plum tomatoes*
2 cups tomato purée, fresh or canned
1 1/2 cups tomato paste
1 cup Beef Stock or Chicken Stock (see recipes)
1 teaspoon dried basil
1 teaspoon dried oregano
1 pinch of ground sage
Salt and freshly ground pepper to taste
1 cup grated Parmesan

Heat the oil in a deep saucepan. Add the garlic and onions, stirring constantly, until the onions are soft but not brown. Add the tomatoes, tomato purée, tomato paste, stock, and all the herbs and seasonings. Simmer over low heat 1 hour, or until the sauce is the right consistency. Add the grated cheese and simmer 20 minutes longer.

Fresh Oysters Mignonette

SERVES 4

In France, chilled raw oysters are *always* served with a mignonette sauce—peppery, with shallot and vinegar. We like to experiment and have included three of our favorite variations on the basic mignonette sauce as well.

2 tablespoons finely minced shallots
3 tablespoons red wine vinegar
1 teaspoon cracked peppercorns
12 oysters, shucked, arranged on the half shell, and chilled

In a small bowl, whisk together the shallots, vinegar, and cracked pepper. Set aside for 30 minutes before serving to allow the flavors to mingle.

To serve, spoon the mignonette sauce over prepared oysters.

NOTE: This recipe can be doubled for larger portions or to serve more people.

Cilantro Mignonette: Add 1 tablespoon minced cilantro (coriander) and 1 teaspoon minced chives to the basic sauce.

Tomato Mignonette: Add 2 tablespoons peeled, seeded, and chopped tomato and 1 finely minced garlic clove to the basic sauce.

Bell Pepper Mignonette: Add 2 tablespoons finely chopped red or green bell pepper to the basic sauce.

Salmon Tartare

SERVES 8 TO 10

1 pound raw salmon fillets
1 tablespoon sour cream
2 tablespoons chopped fresh parsley
1 tablespoon chopped fresh dill, or 1/4 teaspoon dried
4 anchovy fillets, drained, rinsed with cold water, and finely chopped
6 tablespoons minced shallots
4 tablespoons whole capers, drained
2 tablespoons prepared horseradish
2 tablespoons Dijon mustard
4 drops of Tabasco sauce (optional)
2 tablespoons freshly squeezed lemon juice, or more to taste
Salt and freshly ground pepper to taste

Chop the salmon fine and set aside. Combine the sour cream, parsley, dill, anchovies, shallots, capers, horseradish, mustard, and Tabasco, if desired, and stir well. Gently fold this mixture into the chopped salmon, then season with lemon juice, salt, and pepper. Serve with toast or crackers.

Cold Seafood Sausage with Tomato-Basil Vinaigrette

SERVES 10 AS A FIRST COURSE; 4 TO 6 FOR LUNCH

This elegant appetizer, a creation of Chef Pascal Oudin at Dominique's in Miami Beach, can be served as a light lunch or brunch dish as well.

3/4 pound fresh halibut fillets
3/4 pound sole fillets
Zest of 1 lemon, minced
1 garlic clove, minced
1 teaspoon salt
1/2 teaspoon white pepper
1 tablespoon olive oil
1/4 cup heavy cream
1 cup packed fresh spinach leaves (about 3 ounces), well rinsed and coarsely chopped
Sausage casings, soaked for 24 hours in cold water with a dash of vinegar
Tomato-Basil Vinaigrette (see following recipe)
Dill sprigs or basil leaves for garnish

Cut the halibut into 1/2-inch squares, place in a mixing bowl, and set aside. Cut the sole into 1/2-inch squares and place in the bowl of a food processor fitted with the steel blade. Add the lemon zest and garlic and process. Add salt and pepper and process to blend. With motor running, add the olive oil and then the cream through feed tube. Add sole purée and chopped spinach leaves to the reserved halibut and stir well to combine.

With a sausage machine, or a pastry bag if a machine is not available, stuff this mixture into the casings, tying off at intervals of about 4 inches. Twist and tie between the sausages with white kitchen twine. Refrigerate for 30 minutes.

Grill the sausages, then refrigerate until ready to serve.

To serve, spoon the vinaigrette onto chilled salad plates, and place 1 sausage on each plate for a first course, 2 or 3 sausages for lunch. Garnish with the fresh herbs.

NOTE: To prepare this without a food processor, purée the sole in a food mill, and beat in the remaining ingredients.

Tomato-Basil Vinaigrette

MAKES ABOUT 2 CUPS

5 tomatoes, peeled and seeded
1 garlic clove, minced
2 egg yolks
2 tablespoons red wine vinegar
1 teaspoon salt
1/2 teaspoon white pepper
1 cup olive oil
4 fresh basil leaves, chopped (about 2 tablespoons)

Core and quarter 4 tomatoes, and place them in the bowl of a food processor fitted with the steel blade (or in a blender). Add the garlic, egg yolks, vinegar, salt, and pepper and purée. With motor running, add the olive oil in a slow stream to emulsify. Strain through a sieve. Chop the remaining tomato, and blend into the sauce with chopped basil.

Shrimp with Ginger

SERVES 4

Another Miami Beach creation.

12 large raw shrimp, peeled, with tails left on
Salt and freshly ground pepper to taste
2 tablespoons olive oil
2 tablespoons finely chopped fresh ginger
1 tablespoon finely chopped garlic
⅓ cup honey
4 tablespoons red wine vinegar
⅓ cup soy sauce
⅓ cup teriyaki sauce
½ cup Demi-glace or Brown Sauce (see recipe)

Season the shrimp with salt and pepper. In a large skillet, place the olive oil over high heat. When it starts to sizzle, add the shrimp and sauté, turning occasionally, for 5 to 6 minutes. Transfer the shrimp to a warm plate and set in a 250°F. oven to keep warm. Add the ginger and garlic to the skillet and sauté for 2 to 3 minutes over medium heat. Add the honey and boil, stirring occasionally, until it is caramel-colored. Remove the skillet from heat and stir in the red wine vinegar, soy sauce, and teriyaki sauce to deglaze pan. Reduce over high heat and thicken until the sauce coats the back of a spoon. Stir in the demi-glace and strain. Taste and adjust the seasoning as necessary.

To serve, spoon some sauce onto 4 small plates. Top with 3 large shrimp per serving.

Smoked Trout Mousse Canapés

MAKES 50 HORS D'OEUVRES

One 8- to 10-ounce smoked trout or whitefish
¼ cup heavy cream
Salt and freshly ground pepper to taste
1 pinch of ground ginger
Fresh lemon juice to taste
1 to 2 tablespoons grated fresh horseradish
Two 8-ounce packages cream cheese, at room temperature
Fifty ¼-inch slices peeled cucumber
50 cooked baby shrimp
Dill sprigs for garnish

Remove the skin and bones from the smoked trout or whitefish. Place the flesh in the bowl of a food processor fitted with the steel blade and chop finely. Or pass through food mill and transfer to a blender.

With the motor of the processor or blender running, add the cream in a steady stream. Season with salt, pepper, ginger, lemon juice, and horseradish. Beat the cream cheese into the fish mixture until well combined and smooth. Press the mixture through a fine sieve, using a spatula. Refrigerate until ready to use.

With a pastry bag, pipe the chilled mousse onto cucumber slices, and top each with a baby shrimp and fresh dill.

Terrine de Poisson

SERVES 8 TO 10

Another Miami Beach specialty, this must be made a day ahead
and chilled thoroughly.

Juice of 1 medium lemon
½ cup dry white wine
3 tablespoons chopped fresh tarragon
1½ teaspoons salt
1 teaspoon freshly ground white pepper
¾ pound salmon, boned, skinned, and cut into 5-by-½-inch strips
2 tablespoons unsalted butter
¾ cup diced carrots
½ cup diced zucchini
6 large asparagus, trimmed
1 pound scallops
1 egg
¼ teaspoon cayenne
2 cups heavy cream
1 pound spinach, cleaned, with stems removed

In a glass bowl, combine the lemon juice, white wine, 2 tablespoons chopped tarragon, ½ teaspoon salt, and ½ teaspoon
white pepper. Add the salmon, toss to coat, cover, and marinate
in the refrigerator for 2 hours, turning it two or three times.

In a small saucepan, melt the butter over medium heat. Add
the carrots and zucchini and sauté until tender, about 10 minutes. Set aside to cool.

Cook the asparagus in boiling salted water for 5 minutes,
just until tender—*do not overcook.* Drain and reserve.

Preheat the oven to 350°F.

In the bowl of a food processor fitted with the steel blade,
purée the scallops. Add the egg, remaining 1 tablespoon tarra-

gon, 1 teaspoon salt, ½ teaspoon white pepper, and the cayenne and process until smooth. With the motor running, pour in the cream and process until well blended. Transfer the mixture to a large bowl, gently fold in the reserved zucchini and carrots, taste, and adjust the seasoning.

Generously butter an ovenproof terrine or loaf pan. Arrange the spinach leaves on the bottom to a depth of ½ inch, draping the leaves up the sides of the terrine and leaving an overhang at the top. Spoon a 1-inch layer of scallop mousse on the bottom of the terrine, smoothing to create an even layer. Arrange half the asparagus over the mousse, then cover with a thin layer of mousse. Arrange the marinated salmon on top, then add the remaining asparagus. Fill the terrine with the remaining mousse, and fold the overhanging spinach leaves over the mousse to cover.

Butter a piece of aluminum foil and fit it over the terrine, buttered side down. Place the terrine in a baking pan filled with a boiling-water bath to reach halfway up the side of the terrine. Bake 1 hour, or until firm to the touch. Remove from the oven, cool to room temperature, then refrigerate 24 hours.

Slice and serve with a light mayonnaise, mayonnaise blended with minced watercress, or Tomato-Basil Vinaigrette (see recipe).

NOTE: This dish can be prepared in a food mill or blender. To prepare with a food mill, purée the scallops in the food mill, then blend in remaining ingredients per instructions, beating well to ensure a smooth mousse. If using a blender, add the scallops and egg together. If the mixture is too coarse to blend well, add some of the cream to lighten it. Then blend in the seasonings, remaining cream, and proceed with the recipe.

Chicken Liver Fritters

SERVES 4

3/4 pound fresh chicken livers, cleaned and trimmed
1/2 cup Madeira
1 teaspoon Cognac or brandy
Salt and freshly ground pepper to taste
1 cup sifted all-purpose flour
Fritter Batter (see following recipe)
Oil for frying
Soy sauce

Cut livers into 1-inch pieces. Marinate in the Madeira and Cognac for 2 to 3 hours, refrigerated.

Drain the liquid and discard. Dry the livers gently on paper towels. Place the salt, pepper, and flour in a brown paper bag. Add the livers, hold top firmly closed, and shake gently to coat the livers with seasoned flour. Dip the liver pieces in the batter, coating thoroughly. Deep-fry at 360°F. until golden brown. Drain on paper towels.

Place a toothpick in each liver fritter and serve with soy sauce for dipping.

Fritter Batter

MAKES ABOUT 1 CUP

1 cup sifted all-purpose flour
1 teaspoon double-acting baking powder
½ teaspoon salt
1 tablespoon butter, melted
½ cup milk or beer
1 egg plus 1 yolk, beaten lightly
1 egg white, beaten stiff

Sift together the flour, baking powder, and salt in a deep bowl. Combine the melted butter and milk, and stir into the sifted ingredients. Blend well. Add the beaten egg and extra yolk, beating well to eliminate all lumps. Fold the stiffly beaten egg white into the prepared batter. Let stand in a cool place for about 1 hour before using.

Duck Liver Mousse

SERVES 6

Our chefs serve this dish in Miami Beach with toasted French bread, garnished with fresh green vegetables such as asparagus. This needs to be prepared a day or two ahead, so plan accordingly.

1 1/2 pounds duck livers, cleaned and trimmed
1/2 pound chicken livers, cleaned and trimmed
2 tablespoons olive oil
4 medium tart apples, such as McIntosh
4 ounces unsalted butter
1 tablespoon sugar
1/4 pound pistachio nuts, shelled
2 tablespoons Cognac or brandy
Salt and freshly ground pepper to taste

Pat the livers dry with paper towels. Place the olive oil in a saucepan or large skillet over high heat. Add the livers and sauté until firm but still pink in the center, about 3 minutes, stirring constantly with a wooden spoon. Set aside.

Peel and core the apples, and slice them thinly. Melt the butter in a clean skillet and sauté apple slices until tender, 5 to 7 minutes. Add the sugar and raise the heat to high, cooking until the sugar carmelizes and turns golden brown. Remove from the heat.

In the bowl of a food processor fitted with the steel blade, purée the livers, apples, pistachios, and Cognac; or purée all in a food mill or blender. Season with salt and pepper to taste, then spoon into 6 individual 1/2-cup ramekins or molds. Cover and refrigerate overnight. (This mousse may be made 2 days in advance, if desired.)

Remove the molds from the refrigerator 30 minutes before serving and unmold, if desired, by dipping the molds briefly in hot water, running a spatula or knife carefully around the edges, then inverting them onto serving plates.

Fresh Foie Gras Terrine

SERVES 8 TO 10

Another liver dish popular in the Miami Beach Dominique's, this is the king of kings, expensive but well worth the effort.

Dominique's gets its foie gras from a special farm in New York State, but specialty butchers and gourmet shops frequently carry foie gras or they can order it for you. This dish needs to be prepared a day or more ahead.

2 raw goose livers (about 1 pound each)
1 tablespoon salt
½ teaspoon freshly ground pepper
1 pinch of grated nutmeg
1 pinch of quatre épices, blended (see Note)
1 teaspoon sugar
1 ½ tablespoons port
1 ½ tablespoons sherry
1 ½ tablespoons Armagnac

With your hands, separate the large lobe from the small lobe of each goose liver. Cut each lobe open and, with the point of a small sharp knife, remove the network of veins. Arrange the 4 opened lobes in an ovenproof terrine or baking dish just large enough to hold the livers in one layer. Season with salt, pepper, nutmeg, quatre épices, and sugar. Pour the port, sherry, and Armagnac over. Cover, refrigerate, and let marinate for 12 hours, turning once or twice.

Remove the terrine from refrigerator 1 hour before cooking. Arrange the liver lobes as near to their original shape as possible, pressing down firmly.

Preheat the oven to 300°F.

Place the terrine in a hot-water bath to about ¾ inch high. Cook 40 minutes. Remove from the oven and let cool to room temperature. Refrigerate, covered, for 24 hours before serving.

Serve the fois gras thinly sliced, accompanied by buttered toasted French bread and dry Chablis, champagne, or a very rich sweet wine. Or, serve on a bed of greens, if you wish, with cooked imported mushrooms such as chanterelles or cèpes.

NOTE: To make quatre épices, a blend of 4 spices used in pâtés, meat loaves, terrines, and hearty meat dishes, combine 1 teaspoon each ground cloves, ground nutmeg, and ground ginger with 1 tablespoon ground cinnamon, and store, tightly covered, until needed.

Buffalo Sausages

SERVES 8

This appetizer is a favorite of dancer-director Mikhail Barysh-
nikov, a special guest of ours at Dominique's. This needs to be
begun two days ahead.

1 1/2 pounds buffalo meat, top round
1/2 pound veal liver, membranes removed
1/2 pound pork fatback
3/4 pound pork loin
1 tablespoon salt
1/2 teaspoon freshly ground pepper
1/2 teaspoon freshly grated nutmeg
1 pinch of allspice
1 1/2 tablespoons Madeira
1 1/2 tablespoons Cognac or brandy
3 to 4 sprigs thyme
4 shallots, chopped
1/4 pound sausage casings preserved in salt
Unsalted butter and oil for sautéing
Red Wine Sauce with Thyme (see recipe)

To prepare the sausages, cut the buffalo, veal liver, pork fatback,
and pork loin into 1-inch strips. Put them in a bowl with salt,
pepper, nutmeg, and allspice and stir to distribute the seasonings. Add the Madeira, Cognac, thyme sprigs, and shallots.
Cover tightly and refrigerate for 48 hours, stirring two or three
times.

Soak the sausage casings in cold water acidulated with vinegar overnight. Drain.

In a meat grinder with a medium-size blade, insert the
stuffing funnel, attach the sausage casings, fill the hopper with
the meat mixture, and very slowly grind the meat and stuff the

casings, twisting and tying off the sausages to the size of your choice with kitchen twine.

To cook the sausages, prick them in two or three places with a two-tined fork. Place in a large pot of barely simmering water and poach until the water boils. Remove the pot from the heat and let the sausages cool in the water. Drain well. Sauté the sausages in equal amounts of unsalted butter and oil, browning them slowly to prevent bursting. Serve immediately, sliced thickly, with Red Wine Sauce with Thyme.

Marinated Goat Cheese

SERVES 4

1 1/2 cups good-quality olive oil
1 bay leaf
6 peppercorns, crushed
1 tablespoon dried thyme
4 Crottin or four 1/2-inch slices of Montrachet or other good-quality goat
*   cheese*
3/4 cup chopped fresh basil
6 garlic cloves, peeled, halved, and crushed
4 tablespoons chopped fresh parsley

Blend the olive oil, bay leaf, peppercorns, and thyme in a saucepan over medium heat, stirring, for 3 minutes. Place cheese in a glass baking dish and add the oil mixture, basil, garlic, and parsley. Cover and refrigerate overnight.

Serve cold, or heated in a moderate oven, on spinach or lettuce leaves. Pour marinade over all.

Potato Pancakes

MAKES 8 PANCAKES

6 medium baking potatoes (about 2 pounds)
2 eggs, at room temperature
1/3 cup finely grated onion
1/3 cup sifted all-purpose flour
1 pinch of freshly ground pepper
1 teaspoon salt
8 to 10 tablespoons of bacon fat or lard
Applesauce

Peel potatoes and drop them in cold water to prevent discoloring. Beat eggs with a fork in a large round-bottomed bowl; add onion and gradually stir in flour, pepper, and salt.

Drain the potatoes and pat dry. Grate each one coarsely into a colander. One handful at a time, squeeze out their water content. Once the water content has been removed, stir into the egg and onion mixture.

Preheat oven to 275°F.

In a medium cast-iron skillet melt bacon fat or lard over high heat. As soon as the grease starts to sizzle, pour in about 1/3 cup of potato mixture. With a spatula, flatten the potato mixture into a pancake about 4 to 5 inches in diameter. Cook over medium heat for about 2 minutes on each side or until golden brown on both sides. Transfer to a heated platter, and keep in oven until ready to serve. Continue making pancakes with the remaining batter, adding more fat if needed to keep a depth of about 1/4 inch in the pan.

Serve with applesauce.

Linguine with Wild Mushrooms

SERVES 4

This dish must be made at the last minute, but it's simple and takes only minutes to prepare.

1 pound fresh wild mushrooms (morels, chanterelles, or shiitakes, or a
*   combination of 2 or all 3)*
1/2 cup walnut oil
1 shallot, minced
1 garlic clove, minced
Salt and freshly ground pepper to taste
1 cup heavy cream
1 tablespoon sherry
1 sprig thyme, stemmed
1 sprig tarragon, stemmed
1 teaspoon chopped fresh basil
1 pound fresh linguine

Clean the mushrooms under cold water, and drain on paper towels. Slice thickly and set aside.

Place the walnut oil in a sauté pan or skillet over high heat. When the oil is hot, add the sliced mushrooms and sauté, stirring constantly, until barely tender. Add the shallot, garlic, salt, and pepper and sauté another minute. Add the cream, sherry, and herbs and let the sauce simmer for 2 minutes to blend the flavors.

Meanwhile, cook the pasta until just *al dente,* not too soft. Drain, and toss with the hot mushroom-cream sauce.

Fettuccine with Tomatoes, Basil, and Garlic

SERVES 4

Serve this as a first course, or with a green salad and bread for a luncheon.

5 garlic cloves, minced
4 tablespoons chopped fresh basil
1 cup cleaned, trimmed, and sliced mushrooms
1 1/2 cups heavy cream
4 medium ripe tomatoes, peeled, seeded, and sliced
1 1/2 pounds fresh fettuccine
Salt and freshly ground pepper to taste
1/3 cup freshly grated Parmesan

Bring a large pot of salted water to a boil. While the water is heating, combine the garlic, basil, mushrooms, and cream in a heavy saucepan. Bring the mixture to a boil and simmer gently, stirring frequently, until the sauce is reduced by one-third and is thick enough to coat the back of a spoon. Turn off the heat and add the tomatoes to the sauce, stirring well to blend.

Cook the pasta until it is just *al dente.* If the pasta is very fresh, it should cook in less than a minute. Drain the fettuccine well, and toss it with the sauce. Add salt and pepper, sprinkle with Parmesan, and serve at once.

Lobster Ravioli

SERVES 4

When I eat this creation of Chef Pascal's, it's my main course. It's very rich and, paired with a Dandelion Salad (see recipe), absolutely divine. Maestro Rostropovich of Washington's National Symphony Orchestra is a fan of this dish. You will be, too, when you try it!

PASTA DOUGH

3 to 4 cups all-purpose flour
1 pinch of salt
3 eggs
1 to 2 tablespoons cold water
2 tablespoons olive oil

1 raw lobster tail (about 1 pound) for garnish (optional)

LOBSTER MOUSSE FILLING

¾ pound cooked fresh lobster meat, chilled
1 egg, chilled
1 teaspoon salt
½ teaspoon freshly ground white pepper
½ teaspoon cayenne
1 cup heavy cream, very cold

1 egg beaten with 2 tablespoons water, as egg wash
Lobster Bisque au Madère (see recipe), simmered to reduce by half

To prepare the pasta, in the bowl of a food processor fitted with a steel blade, or in the bowl of an electric mixer, combine the flour and salt. Add the eggs, water, and olive oil and process or blend until the dough forms a ball. Remove from the work bowl, dust with flour, wrap tightly with plastic wrap, and refrigerate for about 2 hours.

To prepare the optional garniture, steam the lobster tail for about 10 minutes, or until red in color. Chill thoroughly, then remove the meat from the shell and slice vertically into 12 medaillions. Reserve.

To prepare the filling, purée the 3/4 pound cooked lobster meat, egg, salt, white pepper, and cayenne in the bowl of a food processor fitted with a steel blade. (If using a food mill, purée the lobster meat, then proceed with the recipe using a blender.) With the motor running, pour the heavy cream through the feed tube and process until the cream is well incorporated. Adjust the seasoning to taste, cover, and chill until ready to use.

To assemble the ravioli, roll out half the dough very thinly to a rectangle measuring 25 by 4 inches. Brush the dough with the egg wash to cover. Keep the remaining dough wrapped until ready to use. Place 1 teaspoon mousse at even intervals over the surface of the dough in 2 rows of 6 teaspoonfuls each, using half of the mousse mixture. Place the garniture of lobster medaillions, if desired, on the mousse mounds, then top with equal amounts of the remaining mousse. Roll out the remaining dough to the same size, and place gently on top of the mousse mounds. Press the dough firmly around the filling. With a pastry wheel or ravioli cutter, cut into 12 individual ravioli. Let the ravioli sit, covered with a damp towel, in the refrigerator for a few hours.

To cook the ravioli, poach them in boiling salted water to which 1 tablespoon oil has been added. Cook about 5 minutes, or until *al dente.* Drain, and serve with the lobster sauce.

Smoked Salmon with Fettuccine

SERVES 4

2 cups heavy cream
¾ cup freshly grated Parmesan
8 ounces smoked salmon, cut into ½-inch strips
Freshly ground white pepper to taste
1 pound fresh fettuccine
2 tablespoons snipped fresh chives or chopped scallion tops

In a large saucepan, bring the cream to a boil. Turn down the heat and simmer for 3 minutes. Add the Parmesan and stir rapidly with a wooden spoon. Add the salmon and stir gently, cooking for about 1 minute. Season with pepper.

Meanwhile, cook the fettuccine until *al dente,* and drain. Toss the sauce over the fettuccine to coat evenly, and garnish with chives or scallion tops. Serve, if desired, with additional Parmesan.

Soups

Dominique's is known nationwide for its U.S. Senate Bean Soup, sold in cans and in the restaurant. I am including here a more luxurious version than that served in the Senate dining room. The basis for the U.S. Senate Bean Soup, and all the soups we serve at Dominique's, is a good fresh stock. You can get by with canned stock when you're in a hurry, but if you prepare the homemade stock recipes that follow you'll make better soup. And since the stocks can be easily frozen for later use, there's no reason to deprive yourself of the fresh flavor a homemade stock provides. So first, before the recipes, some hints about stocks for soups and sauces.

We start out with the basic stocks, which are fundamental to any French cook. I have tried to provide very simple versions of what can be complicated and time-consuming preparations. My Simple Chicken Stock, for example, requires the simplest cooking of all ingredients in a stockpot for 2 hours. However, before you begin, read these hints and suggestions to ensure success with your stock making.

- Stockpots should be made of thick aluminum. It is best to use a narrow, deep pot, so evaporation won't be too rapid. Choose a pot that will be nearly filled to the top by the stock mixture, so it will be easy to skim.

- Skimming is done as the stock comes to a boil. Skim immediately and often, discarding the foam that rises to the top. This must be done frequently as the stock cooks, in order to provide a clear broth.

- The color of your stock will depend on the ingredients. Chicken and veal stock will be pale and beige, beef stock will be a medium brown color.

- Once stock has been prepared, chill it to allow any remaining fat to congeal on the surface, at which time it can be easily skimmed. If you do not have time to chill the stock before using it, degrease it by drawing paper towels quickly across the surface to absorb any remaining fat floating there.

- Beef and veal stock can be kept for several weeks in the refrigerator, provided you boil them for 10 minutes once every 3 days. Fish and chicken stock must be boiled every 2 days.

- Stock can be frozen very successfully. To save freezer space, reduce the stock to concentrate, then freeze in an oiled ice cube tray, transferring frozen cubes to a plastic bag for storage. Dilute the cubes as needed with water to reconstitute stock.

The stock recipes all call for a popular seasoning blend called *bouquet garni,* a tied bundle of herbs that you can prepare fresh or purchase dried. To make your own, tie up with string or place in a small mesh spice bag the following: a few sprigs of parsley, a bay leaf, and a sprig of thyme. The bouquet garni is removed at the end of cooking and discarded.

Beef Stock

MAKES 2 TO 3 QUARTS

Used for rich brown sauces and meat and game dishes, this mellow stock may be prepared entirely with veal bones for a heartier flavor.

2 pounds beef bones, cracked or cut into pieces
2 pounds veal bones, cracked or cut into pieces
2 onions, quartered
2 carrots, quartered
2 celery stalks with leaves, cut into 2-inch pieces
1 bouquet garni (see p. 32)
10 peppercorns
1 garlic clove, unpeeled
3 to 4 quarts water
1 tablespoon tomato paste
½ onion, for color (optional)

Preheat the oven to 450°F.

Put the bones in a roasting pan and bake, stirring occasionally, 30 to 40 minutes, or until browned. Add the vegetables and continue roasting until they are brown and the bones are very well colored, another 20 to 30 minutes. Transfer the bones and vegetables to a stockpot, discarding any rendered fat. Add the bouquet garni, peppercorns, garlic, and enough water to cover well. Stir in the tomato paste and bring slowly to a boil, skimming often. Singe the onion half by holding it over a flame on the tines of a fork or in a small skillet, until the cut side is charred. Add it to the stock. Continue simmering 4 to 5 hours, skimming occasionally; the stock should be reduced very slowly.

Strain the stock, discarding all solids. Taste and reduce if a stronger flavor is desired. Store in the refrigerator for up to 4 days, or for several weeks if the stock is boiled for 10 minutes every 3 days. Or freeze for longer storage. Skim any accumulated fat off surface before using.

Chicken Stock

MAKES 2 QUARTS

Chicken stock is used for poultry dishes and many French sauces, and may be substituted for white veal stock.

3 pounds veal bones, cracked or cut into pieces
3 pounds chicken backs and necks, or one 3-pound whole chicken
2 onions, quartered
4 carrots, quartered
4 celery stalks with leaves, cut into 2-inch pieces
1 bouquet garni (see p. 32)
10 peppercorns
2 garlic cloves, unpeeled
4 quarts water, or more as needed

Place the veal bones in a pot of water to cover, bring to a boil, and cook 5 minutes to blanch. Drain, and rinse the bones in cold water. Put the bones, chicken, and vegetables in a stockpot. Add the bouquet garni, peppercorns, and garlic, and add enough water to cover all the ingredients. Bring slowly to a boil, skimming often. Simmer 4 hours, skimming occasionally. If you use a whole chicken that you plan to eat, remove it after 1 ½ hours, or it will be tough. The longer the chicken cooks, however, the more flavor it will impart to the stock.

Strain the stock, discarding all solids. Taste and reduce if a stronger flavor is desired. Cool, refrigerate, and skim off the fat. Store in the refrigerator for up to 4 days, or for 2 weeks if the stock is boiled every 2 days. Or freeze for longer storage.

34

Simple Chicken Stock

MAKES ABOUT 1 1/2 QUARTS

This is a light, quick stock to make when you're in a hurry.

1 1/2 pounds chicken pieces, such as necks, legs, and carcasses
2 celery stalks with leaves, cut up
1 carrot, cut up
1 onion, thinly sliced
1 branch fresh thyme
6 parsley stems
Water to cover

Place all the ingredients in a 2-quart stockpot and cover entirely with cold water. Bring to a boil, reduce heat, and skim the surface of the broth. Simmer gently about 2 hours, skimming occasionally. Strain twice through cheesecloth, discarding all solids. Degrease and use, or store in the refrigerator or freezer.

Fish Stock

MAKES 1 QUART

Fish stock is used in fish soups, for making sauces served with fish or shellfish, and for poaching fish. Don't boil the stock longer than called for in the recipe or it will turn bitter.

1 tablespoon butter
1 medium onion, sliced
1 1/2 pounds fish bones, cut into pieces
1 quart water
10 peppercorns
1 bouquet garni (see p. 32)
1 cup dry white wine

In a large pot, melt the butter and cook the onion slices slowly until soft but not brown, about 7 to 10 minutes. Add the fish bones, water, peppercorns, bouquet garni, and wine. Simmer, uncovered, for 15 minutes. Do not overcook. Strain and cool. Fish stock can be kept for 1 day in the refrigerator, or for several weeks if it is boiled every 2 days. It freezes well for later use.

White Veal Stock

MAKES 2 TO 3 QUARTS

White veal stock is used for soups and for light sauces, sautés, stews, and chicken dishes. It is an all-purpose stock that, because of its neutral flavor, blends with almost any food.

5 pounds veal bones, cracked or cut into pieces
4 onions, quartered
3 carrots, quartered
6 celery stalks with leaves, cut into 2-inch pieces
1 bouquet garni (see p. 32)
10 peppercorns
2 garlic cloves, unpeeled
4 to 5 quarts water

Place the veal bones in a pot of water to cover, bring to a boil, and cook 5 minutes to blanch. Drain, and rinse the bones in cold water. Put the bones and vegetables in a stockpot. Add the bouquet garni, peppercorns, and garlic, and add enough water to cover all ingredients. Bring slowly to a boil, skimming often. Simmer for at least 5 hours, skimming occasionally; the stock should be reduced very slowly.

Strain the stock and let cool. Refrigerate, then skim the fat from surface. The stock will keep, refrigerated, for up to 4 days, or for several weeks if boiled for 10 minutes every 3 days. The stock also freezes well for later use.

Vegetable Broth

MAKES ABOUT 1 QUART

While not strictly a broth, this can be used as a broth, a light soup, or instead of chicken or veal stock in most cases.

1 gallon cold water
3 onions, cut into large pieces
5 celery stalks with leaves, finely sliced
2 carrots, finely sliced
2 leeks, white parts only, washed well and cut into 1-inch slices
2 turnips, peeled and cut into large pieces
1 red pepper, seeded and cubed
1 green pepper, seeded and cubed
4 large tomatoes, cut into chunks
2 branches fresh dill, or 1 teaspoon dried
3 garlic cloves, unpeeled
4 sprigs Italian parsley
1 bay leaf
1 sprig thyme, or 1 teaspoon dried
8 peppercorns

Place all the ingredients in an 8-quart stockpot. Bring to a quick boil, skimming often. Reduce the heat and simmer gently, uncovered, for about 2½ hours.

Strain the stock, discarding all solids. Cool to room temperature, then refrigerate or freeze until ready to use.

U.S. Senate Bean Soup

SERVES 4

We sell several thousand cases of canned U.S. Senate Bean Soup every month, not counting what we serve at the restaurants. Try Dominique's version—more luxurious than the soup actually served in the Senate dining room.

1 pound Michigan navy beans
About 2 quarts Chicken Stock (see recipe)
1 small smoked ham hock
1 cup finely diced onion
½ cup finely diced celery
1 carrot, grated
Salt and freshly ground pepper to taste
2 tablespoons olive oil
4 tablespoons crumbled crisp-cooked bacon

In a large bowl, cover the beans with cold water to a depth of 3 inches and let soak overnight.

The next day, drain the beans and place in a large heavy pot. Cover with the chicken stock and bring to a quick boil. Add the ham hock, onion, celery, and carrot. Skim from time to time to remove scum from surface. Cover and simmer slowly for 4 hours, or until the beans are tender. Remove and discard the ham hock. Season with salt and pepper. Add the olive oil. If the soup is too thick, thin with additional chicken stock.

Just before serving, break the beans by stirring firmly with a large spoon or ladle until the soup becomes cloudy. Serve piping hot, sprinkling individual servings with the crumbled bacon.

Onion Soup Lyonnaise

SERVES 6

This is a thick, rich soup enjoyed at Dominique's by my compatriot Charles Aznavour.

10 tablespoons butter
3 1/2 cups thinly sliced Bermuda onions
1 tablespoon sugar
2 tablespoons all-purpose flour
7 cups Chicken Stock or Beef Stock (see recipes)
1 1/3 cups dry white wine
1 teaspoon salt
1 pinch of pepper
Six 1/2-inch slices of French bread, toasted
2 cups grated Gruyère, mixed with 3 tablespoons grated Parmesan

Melt 8 tablespoons butter in a large saucepan. Add 3 cups sliced onions, cover, and simmer 30 minutes. Add the sugar and flour and cook, stirring, 3 minutes more. Add the stock, wine, salt, and pepper. Simmer 20 minutes, taste, and adjust the seasonings if desired.

Melt the remaining 2 tablespoons butter in a saucepan and add the remaining 1/2 cup sliced onions. Cook, stirring, until the onions are dark brown and crispy. Add to the soup and simmer 5 minutes.

Preheat the oven to 450°F.

Fill 6 individual ovenproof earthenware bowls with soup. Place a piece of toasted bread on top of each and let sit for 1 minute. Then sprinkle liberally with the cheeses, pressing around edges of each bowl. Place the bowls in the oven for approximately 20 minutes, or until the cheese melts and forms an evenly browned crust. Serve immediately.

Light Tomato Soup

SERVES 4

A simple, flavorful soup with hardly any calories at all; very unusual for a French soup!

1/4 cup minced onion
1/4 cup minced carrot
1/4 cup minced celery
2 small garlic cloves, minced
1 1/2 tablespoons unsalted butter
1/4 cup dry white wine
One 1-pound can Italian tomatoes, puréed
2 cups Chicken Stock (see recipe)
1/4 teaspoon dried basil, crumbled
1/8 teaspoon dried thyme, crumbled
Salt and freshly ground pepper to taste

In a heavy skillet, cook the onion, carrot, celery, and garlic in the butter, covered, over medium-low heat for 5 minutes, or until the vegetables are wilted. Add the wine, tomatoes, stock, basil, thyme, and salt and pepper and simmer, stirring occasionally, for 15 minutes.

Let cool slightly, then purée soup in a food processor or blender, and strain it through a fine sieve. Return the soup to the saucepan and reheat over low heat, stirring constantly. This soup may be made ahead and stored in the refrigerator for up to 3 days. It also freezes well.

Winter Vegetable Soup

SERVES 6

2 cups chopped onions
5 tablespoons butter
2 tablespoons all-purpose flour
6 cups Chicken Stock (see recipe)
1 small bunch parsley, tied with string
2 bay leaves
Salt and white pepper to taste
1 1/2 cups diced potatoes
1 cup diced white turnip
1 cup diced celery stalks with leaves
1 cup heavy cream
3 carrots, peeled and julienned
2 large leeks, washed well, trimmed, and julienned
6 large mushrooms, cleaned and sliced thin

In a large saucepan, sauté the onions in 4 tablespoons butter until soft but not brown. Add the flour and cook over medium heat, stirring, about 3 minutes. Gradually stir in the chicken stock, whisking until smooth. Add the parsley, bay leaves, salt, pepper, and potatoes and simmer, uncovered, until the potatoes are almost tender.

Cook the diced turnip in a small amount of salted water, drain, then add to the soup. Add the celery, stir in the heavy cream, taste and adjust the seasoning, then heat to boiling. Remove the parsley and bay leaves and discard.

While the soup is heating, sauté the carrots, leeks, and mushrooms in the remaining 1 tablespoon butter. Ladle the hot soup into bowls, and garnish with the sautéed strips of carrots, leeks, and mushrooms.

Good Fish Soup

SERVES 4

4 tablespoons butter
1 medium onion, finely chopped
2 small carrots, finely sliced
1 leek, white and green parts, washed well and finely chopped
1 celery stalk, finely sliced
1 cup sliced mushrooms
1 large ripe tomato, peeled, seeded, and chopped
4 cups Fish Stock (see recipe) or clam juice
1 cup dry white wine
1 tablespoon fresh lemon juice
1 sprig thyme, or 1/4 teaspoon dried
1 bay leaf
Salt and freshly ground pepper to taste
1 small pinch of saffron, finely crushed (optional)
1 pound fresh white fish fillets, such as catfish, grouper, snapper, cut into
*   1-inch strips*
2 tablespoons chopped fresh parsley
French garlic bread, toasted

Melt 2 tablespoons butter in a large saucepan over medium heat. Add the onion, carrots, leek, and celery, cover, and cook until tender, about 10 minutes. Add the mushrooms and tomato and cook 3 minutes more.

Add the fish stock or clam juice and wine and bring to a boil. Reduce the heat and simmer 3 minutes. Add the lemon juice, thyme, bay leaf, salt, pepper, and saffron, if desired. Simmer 2 minutes more. Add the fish pieces and simmer about 4 minutes, until the fish is firm but tender.

Remove the soup from the heat and discard the bay leaf. Stir in the remaining 2 tablespoons butter and the parsley, taste and adjust the seasoning, and ladle into soup bowls. Serve with toasted French garlic bread.

Crab Gumbo

SERVES 8 TO 10

The crabmeat makes this gumbo very elegant. When served with a salad, it also makes a nice lunch or light dinner meal.

2 tablespoons vegetable oil
1 green pepper, seeded and chopped
2 medium onions, chopped
2 garlic cloves, crushed and chopped
2 celery stalks, diced
One 15-ounce can cut okra, drained
One 20-ounce can Italian tomatoes, drained
3 tablespoons tomato purée
1 teaspoon dried thyme
1 bay leaf
1/3 teaspoon dried savory
1/3 teaspoon dried basil
1/3 teaspoon ground fennel
1 pinch of nutmeg
1 pinch of salt, or to taste
Tabasco sauce or cayenne to taste
2 tablespoons Worcestershire sauce
2 cups clam juice
5 cups Fish Stock (see recipe)
5 cups water
2 cups cooked rice
2 pounds lump crabmeat, picked over

In a skillet, heat the vegetable oil and sauté pepper and onions for 5 minutes over low heat. Place the sautéed vegetables in a large stockpot and add the remaining ingredients except for the cooked rice and crabmeat. Simmer about 1 hour. Add the rice and crabmeat and cook until heated through, about 5 minutes.

Remove the bay leaf and discard. Taste and adjust the seasonings, and serve piping hot.

Lobster Bisque au Madère

SERVES 4

This rich soup can be reduced and used as a lobster sauce over fish or with Lobster Ravioli, as directed in that recipe.

One 1-pound lobster, boiled
5 tablespoons Clarified Butter (see recipe)
1 small onion, chopped
1 small carrot, chopped
1/2 cup dry white wine
3 cups Fish Stock (see recipe)
2 tablespoons tomato paste
2 tablespoons Madeira
Salt and freshly ground pepper to taste
2 tablespoons sifted all-purpose flour
3/4 cup heavy cream
1 tablespoon Cognac or brandy
1/8 teaspoon cayenne

Insert a small knife down the center of the lobster and remove the dark line of intestines. Carefully loosen and remove the meat from body, discarding the stomach and lungs. Pick over the meat to remove any pieces of shell or sandy particles. Save the shells and head. Dice the lobster meat and set aside.

Melt 3 tablespoons clarified butter in a saucepan over medium heat. Add the onion and carrot and cook, stirring occasionally, for 10 minutes, or until the onion is soft but not browned. Meanwhile, crush the lobster shell and head in a mortar and pestle. Add to the onions and carrots and stir to com-

44

bine. Add the white wine and bring to a quick boil. Stir in the fish stock, tomato paste, Madeira, and salt and pepper; return to a boil and cook 10 minutes. Reduce the heat, cover, and simmer an additional 20 minutes.

Strain the lobster stock, pressing firmly on the solids to extract all flavors. Discard the solids.

Over medium heat, melt the remaining 2 tablespoons clarified butter in a small skillet or saucepan. As soon as the butter begins to sizzle, whisk in the flour and stir constantly for 3 minutes, or until mixture starts to brown. Remove from the heat and add gradually to the strained lobster stock, blending well.

Return the stockpot to heat and bring to a boil. Stir in the cream and simmer. Add the Cognac and reserved lobster meat, simmer 2 minutes, add the cayenne, and taste and adjust the seasoning. Serve immediately.

Oyster Bisque

SERVES 4

4 tablespoons butter
2 tablespoons all-purpose flour
2 cups scalded milk
1 celery stalk with leaves, finely chopped
1 small red or green pepper, seeded and finely diced
4 tablespoons finely chopped onion
4 sprigs parsley
1 bay leaf
Salt and freshly ground pepper to taste
2 cups shucked oysters with juice, chopped
1 tablespoon Worcestershire sauce
1 dash of Tabasco sauce (optional)

Melt the butter in a large saucepan. Stir in the flour and cook over medium heat for 2 to 3 minutes. Gradually whisk in the scalded milk and bring to a boil. Add the celery, diced pepper, onion, parsley, bay leaf, and salt and pepper and boil 2 minutes, or until the vegetables are tender. Add the chopped oysters with their juice, the Worcestershire, and Tabasco, if desired. Heat through but *do not boil.* Remove the parsley sprigs and bay leaf and discard. Serve immediately.

Oyster Pan Roast

SERVES 1

A pan roast is hearty enough to serve as a main course with salad and bread. This recipe makes a single serving, since it is better made in small portions. You can double the recipe to make 2 servings at a time, but for a larger number, repeat the recipe as needed. You can increase or decrease the number of oysters, depending on your appetite!

8 freshly shucked oysters
2 tablespoons salted butter
1 tablespoon chili sauce
1 tablespoon Worcestershire sauce
¼ cup oyster liquor
1 pinch of celery salt
1 tablespoon dry white wine
½ cup half-and-half
1 slice of bread, toasted
½ teaspoon paprika for garnish

Place the oysters, 1 tablespoon butter, chili sauce, Worcestershire, oyster liquor, celery salt, and wine in the top half of a double boiler over boiling water. Don't let the top pan touch the water. Whisk or stir constantly for 1 minute, or just until the oysters begin to curl. Add the half-and-half and continue stirring briskly until the liquid reaches a simmer. *Do not boil.*

Place the toasted bread in a soup bowl, then pour the pan roast on top. Float the remaining 1 tablespoon butter on top, dust with paprika, and serve at once.

Variations: In place of the oysters, use one of the following: 5 raw shrimp, shelled and deveined, with tails removed; 8 freshly shucked cherrystone or littleneck clams; ¼ pound fresh lobster meat; 12 raw bay scallops; or 10 freshly bearded mussels in the shell.

Northwest Oyster Stew

SERVES 4

1 pint (or 18) freshly shucked oysters, liquor reserved
1 cup heavy cream
3 cups milk
1 teaspoon salt
1 tablespoon Worcestershire sauce
Cayenne to taste
2 tablespoons butter
Chopped fresh parsley for garnish

In a large saucepan or Dutch oven, simmer the oysters in their liquor over low heat for 3 minutes, or until the edges begin to curl. Add the cream and milk and heat until bubbles form around the edges of the pot, but *do not boil.* Add the salt, Worcestershire, and cayenne. Remove from the heat and stir in the butter. Garnish with chopped parsley.

Diamondback Terrapin Turtle Soup

SERVES 12

This is my own personal recipe, served a couple of times at the restaurant. It's meant for the hunter who might come across a turtle while hunting ducks and geese. A note of warning: In most states turtles are protected by the federal government, so check with your local wildlife agency before killing or purchasing any turtles. Instructions on killing and dressing a live turtle follow the recipe.

1/2 cup butter
4 tablespoons all-purpose flour
1 large onion, finely chopped
1 green pepper, seeded and finely chopped
1 cup finely chopped celery
1/2 cup chopped fresh parsley
3/4 cup finely chopped well-washed leeks
3 garlic cloves, minced
2 1/2 pounds turtle meat, cut into 3/4-inch cubes
Turtle bones, fat extracted from upper and lower shells, and turtle eggs,
*   if any*
2 quarts Beef Stock (see recipe)
1 quart water
1 1/2 cups dry white wine
4 large ripe tomatoes, peeled and seeded
1 meaty ham bone
2 bay leaves
1 tablespoon salt
1/2 teaspoon cayenne
1 sprig thyme, or 1/4 teaspoon dried
1/2 teaspoon ground cloves
1/2 teaspoon ground allspice

1 pinch of mace
1 tablespoon fresh lemon juice
1 tablespoon Worcestershire sauce
1 1/4 cups dry sherry
2 hard-boiled eggs, chopped, for garnish
4 tablespoons chopped chives or scallions for garnish
12 thin lemon slices for garnish

In a large cast-iron or copper stockpot or kettle, melt the butter over low heat. Whisk in the flour and cook, stirring constantly, until lightly browned (the color of peanuts), about 25 minutes. Add the onion, green pepper, celery, parsley, leeks, and garlic, and cook until tender, about 15 minutes. Add the cubed turtle meat, bones, fat, shells, beef stock, water, and wine and bring to a boil. If turtle eggs are available, set aside for later use. Once the soup comes to a boil, lower heat, and add the tomatoes, ham bone, bay leaves, salt, cayenne, thyme, cloves, allspice, mace, lemon juice, and Worcestershire. Bring the soup to a quick boil, then lower the heat and simmer 2 hours, stirring occasionally. Scrape down the sides and bottom of the pot and skim from time to time. Cover the pot and simmer 1 hour longer.

Remove the turtle bones and shells, ham bone, and bay leaves and discard. Add ½ cup sherry and the reserved turtle eggs, bring the soup to a quick boil, and cook 1 minute only. Taste and adjust the seasoning.

To serve, place 1 tablespoon of the remaining sherry in each bowl. Ladle soup into the bowls, sprinkle with chopped hard-boiled eggs and chives or scallions, and float a lemon slice on top. Serve at once. Leftover ungarnished soup can be frozen.

What to Do if You Have a Live Turtle

Remember the warning above—make sure it's legal before you kill or purchase a turtle. Also, be careful when handling turtles—they snap!

First, fill a large pan (large enough to hold the turtle) with cold water and lots of salt (about 1 tablespoon to each quart of water). Let the live turtle play in water for 3 hours; this is necessary to allow turtle to relax and clean itself. Then, place the turtle on a chopping block and wait; eventually, the turtle will stick out its head. With a single quick motion of a sharp knife or hatchet, decapitate the turtle at the base of the neck. The turtle will die immediately.

Return the turtle to the salted water and let sit for 45 minutes to drain the blood. Rinse the turtle under cold running water, scrub the shell with a hard brush, then rinse again. Weigh the turtle to figure cooking time: 5 minutes per pound of meat. Place the turtle in boiling water and cook until tender, according to the calculated time. Remove from the pot and let cool. Cut off the toenails, and skin the legs and feet. Remove the top and bottom shells, using a strong knife if necessary, being very careful. Lift the top shell without breaking the gallbladder (it is attached to the liver). Discard the gallbladder. Remove the liver and discard, or reserve and cook it for breakfast. Remove the eggs, if any, and refrigerate. Clean out and discard the guts, heart, and all white muscle tissue. Remove all the meat from the body and legs, rinse with cold water, cut into ¾-inch cubes, and refrigerate. Save the bones for soup. Scrape and reserve the greenish fat inside the upper and lower shells, refrigerating until ready to use.

By now you should have the head and neck of the turtle in the garbage can; the liver refrigerated until breakfast; the fat, eggs, and cubed meat reserved in the refrigerator; bones reserved for soup.

If you decide to save the upper shell for a decoration or to display as a souvenir (Dominique's has several!), it should be boiled and scraped clean, then sprayed with clear varnish.

Cream of Artichoke Soup

SERVES 4

3 large artichokes
4 tablespoons butter
1 tablespoon all-purpose flour
2 1/2 cups Chicken Stock (see recipe)
1 cup heavy cream
1 tablespoon minced fresh parsley
1 teaspoon fresh lemon juice
1/2 teaspoon salt
1/4 teaspoon white pepper

In a large stainless-steel pan, bring 2 quarts water to a boil. Trim the stem ends of the artichokes and rinse well. Salt the water and add artichokes. Cover and simmer 35 to 45 minutes, until the artichokes are tender. Invert the artichokes in a colander and let drain until cool enough to handle. Pull the leaves off, scrape off edible flesh, remove the heart and place in the bowl of a food processor with the scrapings. Purée until smooth, adding a little of the stock, if necessary. The heart and scrapings can be puréed in a blender if a food processor is not available.

In a saucepan, melt the butter and add the flour, stirring over low heat, for about 3 minutes to cook the flour. Whisk in the stock and cream and simmer over low heat. Add the parsley, lemon juice, salt, pepper, and artichoke purée. Simmer 5 minutes. Serve very hot.

Cold Avocado Cream Soup

SERVES 4 AS A MAIN COURSE; 6 AS A FIRST COURSE

Very popular in the Miami Beach Dominique's, this soup is rich enough to eat as a main course with a salad or vegetable.

4 very ripe avocados
Juice of 2 lemons
1 quart light cream
Salt and freshly ground pepper to taste
1 pinch of cayenne, or more to taste
1 dash of Worcestershire sauce
1/2 cup fresh croutons (cubed white bread sautéed in 4 tablespoons butter)
    for garnish
1 tablespoon chopped fresh dill for garnish

Peel and pit the avocados. Place them in a blender and purée to a frothy consistency. Slowly, with motor running, add the lemon juice. Blend in the cream, salt, pepper, cayenne, and Worcestershire. To increase the spiciness of the soup, add another dash of cayenne, if desired.

Serve the soup in chilled bowls, topped with croutons and chopped dill.

Lettuce and Chive Cream Soup

SERVES 6

4 cups Chicken Stock (see recipe)
½ cup chopped scallions
10 large Boston lettuce leaves
1 large baking potato, peeled and cubed
1 small onion, quartered
½ cup chopped celery
1 small parsnip, sliced thick, or 1 leek, white only, sliced thick
½ teaspoon grated nutmeg
2 tablespoons chopped fresh parsley
½ cup heavy cream
Salt and freshly ground pepper to taste
6 tablespoons sour cream for garnish
4 tablespoons finely chopped fresh chives for garnish

Combine the chicken stock, scallions, lettuce leaves, potato, onion, celery, and parsnip or leek in a 2-quart saucepan over high heat. Bring to a quick boil, reduce heat, and simmer gently about 45 minutes, or until all the vegetables are tender. Strain. Set liquid aside.

Purée the vegetables in a food mill or food processor. Blend the puréed vegetables with the reserved broth. Add the nutmeg and parsley. Bring the soup to a boil. Reduce the heat and add the cream, stirring gently with a whisk to blend all the ingredients. Add salt and pepper.

Serve hot or cold, garnishing each serving with 1 tablespoon sour cream and with chopped chives.

Scallop or Mussel Chowder

SERVES 6

3 tablespoons butter
1/2 cup diced onion
1/2 cup diced celery
1 1/2 cups sliced mushrooms
2 medium potatoes, peeled and diced
3 3/4 cups clam juice
1 cup milk or light cream
1/4 cup dry sherry
Salt and freshly ground pepper to taste
1/2 cup freshly grated Parmesan
2 tablespoons cornstarch, dissolved in 4 tablespoons clam juice
3/4 pound drained raw scallops or mussels, cleaned, beards removed, and
removed from shells
French garlic bread, toasted

Melt the butter in a large frying pan. Add the onion and celery and cook over medium heat for 5 minutes. Add the mushrooms, potatoes, and clam juice. Bring to a boil, cover, and simmer gently until the potatoes are tender, about 15 minutes. Remove the cover and add the milk or cream, sherry, salt, pepper, and Parmesan and stir to blend. Add the dissolved cornstarch, bring to a slow boil, then add the scallops or mussels. Simmer about 5 minutes, or until the fish is cooked through and tender. Taste and adjust the seasoning.

Serve with toasted garlic bread and pass around additional cheese, if you wish.

Cream of Zucchini Soup

SERVES 4

This very simple zucchini soup can be served either warm or ice cold. The corn at the bottom of the bowl is a pleasant surprise, and lots of freshly cracked black pepper floating on the top is essential.

3 medium zucchini
2 cups light cream
1 teaspoon salt
2 to 6 drops Tabasco sauce, according to taste
1 ear corn
Freshly cracked black pepper

Wash the zucchini, cut into large chunks, and steam until soft. Purée in a blender, and add the cream, salt, and Tabasco to taste, blending well.

Steam the corn for 10 minutes, or until the kernels come away from cob easily. Divide the kernels into 4 soup bowls, and ladle soup into bowls. Top with cracked pepper and serve.

To serve the soup cold, prepare the soup and corn and refrigerate separately until both are very cold. Proceed with the recipe.

Buffalo Soup

SERVES 4 TO 6

This is one of Dominique's popular Washington, D.C., dishes. It's easy to make, once you find the buffalo bones!

4 pounds buffalo bones, such as knucklebone or shanks and neck bones, if available
2 medium onions, sliced
2 carrots, julienned
3 celery stalks, chopped
1 green pepper, seeded and chopped
2 bay leaves
2 tablespoons fresh lemon juice
½ pound fresh angel hair pasta
Salt and freshly ground pepper to taste
1 tablespoon chopped fresh parsley
Freshly grated Parmesan

Cover the bones with cold water in a large stockpot, bring to a boil, reduce heat, and simmer 1 hour or longer, skimming often. Add the vegetables, bay leaves, and 1 tablespoon lemon juice and simmer another hour, or until the meat is tender. Remove the bay leaves and discard. Remove the bones. If a hearty soup is desired, remove the meat from bones and add it to the soup. Discard the bones.

At this point, there should be 2 quarts liquid. Add the angel hair pasta and boil 1 minute, or until the pasta is cooked. Remove from the heat, taste and adjust the seasoning, and stir in the parsley and the remaining 1 tablespoon lemon juice. Sprinkle with Parmesan before serving.

Vegetables

Some years ago, an old friend, the famous French chef René Verdon, suddenly quit his job as White House chef, a post he'd held during the Kennedy administration. It seems that when Lyndon Johnson assumed the presidency, an efficiency expert was brought into the White House kitchen to trim costs. One of the expert's first recommendations was to order the staff to substitute frozen vegetables for fresh!

At Dominique's, just three blocks from the White House, we use only the freshest ingredients in all our recipes. We inspect the vegetables and lettuces carefully when they arrive each morning to ensure that our guests get the best. We vary the vegetable dishes used as garniture with our numerous meat and seafood dishes, depending on what is seasonal, fresh, and good. Some recipes, such as Red Cabbage and Fried Grapes, are natural accompaniments to game meats, while Dominique's Bouquets of Fresh Vegetables successfully garnish almost any entrée. I recommend that you experiment with different combinations, trusting your taste and imagination.

Chinese Bean Sprouts

SERVES 4

We serve these as a garniture with swordfish in both restaurants.

5 cups fresh bean sprouts
¼ cup peanut oil
3 scallions, cut into 2-inch lengths
Salt and freshly ground pepper to taste
1 teaspoon soy sauce
2 teaspoons rice wine vinegar

Soak the bean sprouts in cold water overnight. Rinse them several times in cold water, drain, and dry on paper towels.

Heat the oil in a large heavy skillet. When it sizzles, add the sprouts and scallions. Stir-fry quickly over high heat for 1 minute. Add the salt, pepper, and soy sauce. Cook, stirring, 1 minute more. Add the vinegar and stir-fry another minute. *Do not overcook*—bean sprouts should be crunchy, not mushy. Serve immediately.

Red Cabbage

SERVES 4

This recipe can be prepared a day or two in advance. It improves with aging! Serve with game or sausage.

2 pounds red cabbage
6 tablespoons butter
1 large onion, sliced
3/4 cup water
1 cup dry white wine
1/3 cup red wine vinegar
1 pinch of sugar
2 red apples, cored, peeled, and thinly sliced
Salt and freshly ground pepper to taste
Juice of 1 lemon

Shred the cabbage. Heat the butter in a large skillet over medium heat, add the sliced onion, and cook until tender but not brown. Add the cabbage and cook an additional 5 minutes.

Transfer the contents of the skillet to a large saucepan. Add the water, wine, vinegar, and sugar. Cover and simmer over low heat for 1 hour.

Add the apples and stir to blend. Add salt and pepper. Add the lemon juice and simmer 30 minutes more, or until the cabbage is tender.

Carrot Mousse

SERVES 8

In our restaurants, this dish is served with Veal Medaillions with Morel Sauce.

2 pounds carrots, peeled
4 tablespoons butter
1 pinch of salt
1 pinch of freshly ground pepper
8 eggs, lightly beaten
1 quart heavy cream

Preheat the oven to 350°F.

Slice the carrots, then cook them in a frying pan in 2 tablespoons butter. Once the carrots have softened, purée them in a blender until smooth. Sieve the purée, and season with the salt and pepper. Pour the purée into a mixing bowl and stir to cool.

Once the purée has cooled completely, add the eggs and the cream. Whisk the mixture until it stiffens. Return the mixture to the blender and purée until very smooth.

Lightly grease 8 individual ramekins with the remaining 2 tablespoons butter, and fill the molds with the carrot mixture. Place the ramekins in a roasting pan, pour in enough boiling water to come halfway up their sides, then bake 30 minutes. Serve hot in the ramekins, or unmold before serving.

To prepare ahead, make the carrot mousse and fill the ramekins, then cover and refrigerate. When ready to use, cook 30 minutes, uncovered, as per recipe.

Fried Grapes

SERVES 4 TO 6

These are good with any game bird, even your Thanksgiving turkey!

2 cups seedless green grapes
½ cup all-purpose flour
2 eggs, lightly beaten
1 cup fresh bread crumbs
1 cup vegetable oil, for frying
½ teaspoon paprika

Rinse the grapes under cold water and separate from the stems. Do not dry. Roll the damp grapes in the flour, dip in the eggs, and toss in the bread crumbs, taking care to coat the grapes evenly.

Heat the oil in a deep frypan to 375°F. Deep-fry the grapes for 12 seconds, or until lightly browned. Remove the grapes and drain on paper towels. Dust with paprika and serve.

Baked Leeks

SERVES 4

This is a vegetable that is very much appreciated in France.

4 medium leeks
¼ cup olive oil
Salt and freshly ground pepper to taste
4 tablespoons butter, melted
½ cup dry white wine
4 tablespoons finely chopped celery leaves
Juice of 1 lemon
¼ cup freshly grated Parmesan

Preheat the oven to 425°F.

Trim the roots and tops of the leeks, leaving about 1 inch of the green part. The trimmed leeks should be about 6 inches long. Make an incision the length of each leek, halfway through the center. Soak the leeks in cold water, changing the water at least three times, then hold them under cold running water, 1 at a time, to rinse away all sand and grit. Dip the leeks in the olive oil, and season with salt and pepper. With the incisions facing up, place the leeks in a baking pan. Brush with the melted butter. Add the wine and chopped celery leaves. Cover and bake about 45 minutes, or until tender. Remove from the oven, squeeze lemon juice over, and sprinkle with cheese. Serve at once.

Mushrooms Bordelaise

SERVES 4 TO 6

We serve this with Buffalo Sausages as an entrée; these mushrooms are delicious with all meats and game.

2 pounds fresh mushrooms, preferably wild
½ cup olive oil
4 garlic cloves, chopped
½ cup chopped celery leaves
Salt and freshly ground pepper to taste
4 tablespoons chopped fresh parsley

Wash the mushrooms in cold water. Cut off the stems almost level with the caps, and discard the trimmings. Heat the oil in a large skillet. Brown the mushrooms over high heat for a few minutes. Lower the heat and add all the remaining ingredients except the parsley. Simmer gently until the mushrooms are tender but still on the firm side. Add the parsley. Taste and adjust the seasoning. Serve very hot.

Baked Onions with Vinegar

SERVES 4

We make these onions in the restaurant to serve with smoked trout. I also like them with smoked salmon.

2 large yellow onions
2 large red onions
Salt and freshly ground pepper to taste
5 tablespoons olive oil
4 thin lemon slices
3 tablespoons red wine vinegar
4 tablespoons finely chopped coriander (cilantro) or fresh parsley

Preheat the oven to 375°F.

Remove the outside skin of the onions, leaving the thin inner skin intact. Quarter the onions. Place in an oiled baking pan large enough to accommodate them in a single layer. Dust with salt and pepper. Pour the oil over, add the lemon slices, cover with aluminum foil, and bake 35 minutes. Uncover and bake another 20 minutes, or until the onions are tender.

Transfer the onions to a serving platter. Add the vinegar to the baking dish and heat on top of stove. Bring to a simmer, then pour immediately over the onions. Sprinkle with chopped coriander or parsley. Cool to room temperature, turning occasionally, and serve.

Baked Onions with Cheese

SERVES 4

6 yellow onions
1 cup Beef Stock (see recipe), or more as needed
Salt to taste
1 cup grated Swiss cheese

Preheat the oven to 400°F.

Peel the onions and cut in half crosswise. Lay the onions, flat side down, in a baking dish just large enough to hold them in a single layer. Pour in enough beef stock to reach halfway up the sides of the onions. Sprinkle lightly with salt. Cover and bake about 45 minutes, or until the onions are soft, basting once or twice during baking. Add more stock if too much liquid is evaporating.

Preheat the broiler.

Lift the cooked onions from their baking dish, place in shallow baking pan, and sprinkle with the grated Swiss cheese. Broil for a minute or so, until the tops are a rich golden color.

Sauerkraut with Fresh Apples

SERVES 4 TO 6

1 1/2 pounds sauerkraut
1/3 cup sliced onion
3 tablespoons butter or bacon fat
3 apples, cored, peeled, and sliced
3/4 cup dry white wine
1 1/3 cups Chicken Stock (see recipe)
1 pinch of brown sugar
1/2 teaspoon caraway seeds

Preheat the oven to 325°F.

Rinse and drain the sauerkraut. In a large ovenproof skillet, sauté the onion in butter or bacon fat until tender but not browned. Add the sauerkraut and cook over medium heat for 10 minutes. Add the apples, wine, and chicken stock and cook an additional 20 minutes. Add the brown sugar and caraway seeds, cover, place in the oven, and bake 25 minutes, or until the sauerkraut is tender.

Spinach Soufflé

SERVES 4 TO 6

You can serve this with lightly poached eggs and Parmesan for a hearty brunch or lunch.

1 pound fresh spinach
3/4 cup milk
1/2 cup light cream
4 tablespoons all-purpose flour, mixed with 4 tablespoons milk
4 tablespoons freshly grated Parmesan
Salt and freshly ground pepper to taste
1 pinch of ground nutmeg
4 egg yolks
6 egg whites

Preheat the oven to 375°F.

Generously butter a 2-quart soufflé dish, and dust with flour. Place the dish in the refrigerator.

Clean the spinach and cut off the stems. Rinse in cold water at least three times to remove sand and dirt. Boil 2 quarts water. Drop in the spinach and boil gently for 5 minutes. Remove from the heat and drain the spinach. When the spinach returns to room temperature, squeeze with your hands to remove as much water as possible. You will end up with about 1½ cups cooked spinach.

Place the spinach in a blender and blend to a thin purée, adding the milk. Add the light cream and blend again. Pour the creamy mixture into a saucepan. Add the flour mixture, Parmesan, salt, pepper, and nutmeg. Cook 5 to 6 minutes over medium-high heat, stirring constantly with a whisk, until the mixture thickens. Remove from heat and let cool to room temperature.

Place the mixture in a deep round bowl. Add the egg yolks,

1 at a time, mixing well after each addition. In another bowl, beat the egg whites until stiff but not dry. Whisk one-third of the egg whites gradually but quickly into the spinach mixture to lighten it. Gently fold in the remaining egg whites. Scoop the mixture into the prepared soufflé dish and bake 25 minutes, or until done. Serve immediately.

Spinach Flan

SERVES 4

This Miami Beach special can be served as an appetizer or as a garniture with an entrée such as fish or meat.

3/4 pound fresh spinach, cleaned, with stems removed
1 garlic clove, minced
3 tablespoons unsalted butter
1/2 cup milk
1/2 cup heavy cream
3 eggs
1 teaspoon salt
Freshly ground pepper to taste
1 pinch of ground nutmeg

Preheat the oven to 400°F.

Sauté the spinach and garlic in the butter for 1 minute. Remove from the heat and let cool. Place the spinach on a chopping board and chop coarsely. Set aside.

In a bowl, combine the milk, cream, eggs, salt, pepper, and nutmeg. Add the sautéed spinach and mix well.

Butter 4 individual ramekins. Fill them with the spinach mixture. Place the molds in a roasting pan, pour enough boiling water around them to reach halfway up the sides, and cover with aluminum foil. Bake 20 minutes, or until the flans are firm to the touch.

Pan-Baked Tomatoes
with Fresh Herbs

SERVES 4

4 medium ripe tomatoes with stems
4 tablespoons olive oil
Salt and freshly ground pepper to taste
4 tablespoons extra-virgin olive oil
2 garlic cloves, minced
4 tablespoons coarsely chopped fresh parsley
4 tablespoons coarsely chopped fresh basil
4 branches celery leaves for garnish

Rinse the tomatoes under cold water, leaving the stems intact. Pour 4 tablespoons olive oil into a deep skillet. Place tomatoes in a single layer in the skillet, stem side down. Cook over medium-low heat for 10 to 12 minutes. Dust with salt and pepper. Turn the tomatoes, stems up, reduce the heat to low, and cook 1 hour and 45 minutes.

In a separate pan, heat the extra-virgin olive oil, garlic, parsley, and basil over medium-high heat. Reduce the heat to low and cook about 10 minutes.

Gently transfer the tomatoes to a serving platter. Pour the garlic and herb mixture on top. Place a branch of celery leaves on the top of each tomato. Serve hot or cold.

Cherry Tomatoes
Provençal

SERVES 4

This is a popular garniture at Dominique's. It's also a great way to use up overripe tomatoes.

3 tablespoons olive oil
32 cherry tomatoes, rinsed and stemmed
4 tablespoons finely chopped fresh parsley or a mixture of chopped parsley
*   and chopped fresh basil, oregano, or thyme*
Salt and freshly ground pepper to taste

In a large skillet over medium heat, heat the oil until it sizzles. Add the tomatoes and sauté, stirring occasionally, about 2 or 3 minutes, or until the tomatoes are soft. Sprinkle with the fresh herbs, toss to coat, and season with salt and pepper. Serve hot or cold.

Dominique's Bouquets
of Fresh Vegetables

SERVES 4 TO 6

These bouquets dress up the simplest dish and go well with everything. They're especially attractive alongside a piece of grilled or baked fish.

2 pounds fresh vegetables (a combination of string beans, snow peas,
carrots, red and yellow peppers, broccoli, celery)
2 tablespoons lemon juice
1 ½ tablespoons salt
6 tablespoons butter
½ cup chopped fresh parsley
2 tablespoons chopped fresh tarragon
Salt and freshly ground pepper to taste
1 leek, rinsed well and trimmed
Freshly grated Parmesan

Wash all the vegetables in cold water. Cut off the ends of the string beans and snow peas and remove the strings, if any. Cut the peppers and carrots into julienne strips about 2 inches long. Cut the broccoli into ½-inch-thick florets, discarding the stems. Cut the celery into julienne strips about 1 ½ inches long.

Drop the vegetables into 3 quarts boiling water to which 1 tablespoon lemon juice and 1 ½ tablespoons salt have been added. When the water returns to a boil, reduce the heat and boil slowly about 3 to 5 minutes, until vegetables are crunchy but tender. (Some of the vegetables will cook quicker than others; watch carefully.) Refresh under cold water and drain thoroughly in a colander.

Melt 2 tablespoons butter in a saucepan over medium heat. Add the vegetables and sauté slowly. When the moisture has evaporated, add 2 more tablespoons butter, the remaining 1 tablespoon lemon juice, the parsley, tarragon, and salt and pepper to taste.

Separate the leek leaves and blanch them in boiling water for about 30 seconds. Slice the leeks into long ¼-inch-thick strips. Take 1 or 2 pieces of each vegetable and lay them across the center of a leek piece. Tie the leek around the vegetables, making a bouquet. Cut off any extra leek ends after tying the knot.

Preheat the broiler.

Place the vegetable bouquets on a baking sheet and sprinkle with the Parmesan. Dot with remaining 2 tablespoons butter. Set under the broiler until golden brown, or bake in a preheated 425°F. oven about 10 minutes. Serve immediately.

Potatoes Boulangère

SERVES 4

In French cooking *boulangère,* baker's style, means that a combination of potatoes and onions is included in the dish.

1 pound potatoes
1 medium onion, sliced
Chopped fresh or dried thyme to taste
Salt and freshly ground pepper to taste
2 cups Beef Stock (see recipe)
4 tablespoons chopped fresh parsley for garnish

Preheat the oven to 375°F.

Peel the potatoes and slice them into ¼-inch rounds. Layer a deep 9-inch pie plate or similar ovenproof dish with half the onion slices and then half the potatoes. Sprinkle lightly with thyme, salt, and pepper. Add the remaining onions and potatoes, and repeat the seasoning.

Pour the beef stock over the layered vegetables, to just barely cover. Be sure to pour the stock into the side of the pan in order to not disturb the seasoning on the potatoes. Cover the dish, place in the preheated oven, and bake 45 minutes. Remove the cover and bake another 15 minutes, or until the potatoes can be pierced easily with a sharp knife.

Dust with chopped parsley and serve from the baking dish, spooning a little of the broth from the pan over each portion.

New-Potato Casserole

SERVES 4

We vary our potato side dishes at Dominique's, and serve them
with steaks, fillets, and roasted meats.

1 ½ pounds new potatoes (about 18 small)
½ cup sliced scallions or chives
1 pound Muenster or mozzarella cheese, in thin slices
4 eggs
½ cup milk
½ teaspoon freshly ground pepper
⅓ cup seasoned dry bread crumbs

Preheat the oven to 375°F.

Scrub the potatoes well. Steam them in 1 inch boiling salted
water 20 to 25 minutes, until tender. Rinse in cold water, then
slice thinly.

Butter a 7 ½-by-11 ½-inch baking dish. Arrange one-third
of the potatoes in the dish, top with half the scallions and half
the cheese. Repeat the layers, ending with the potatoes.

In a small bowl, beat together the eggs, milk, and pepper,
and pour over the potatoes. Sprinkle the top evenly with bread
crumbs. Cover and bake 25 minutes. Remove the cover and bake
10 to 15 minutes longer, until the potatoes are tender.

Potatoes Savoyarde

SERVES 4

2 pounds boiling potatoes, peeled and thinly sliced
4 tablespoons unsalted butter
Salt and white pepper to taste
1 1/4 cups grated Gruyère or Swiss cheese
2/3 cup Beef Stock (see recipe)
1 egg
1/2 cup sour cream
1/2 cup heavy cream
2 tablespoons chopped fresh parsley or chives for garnish

Preheat the oven to 425°F.

Drop the sliced potatoes into a pot of cold water, bring to a boil, and cook 10 minutes. Drain the potatoes and dry on paper towels.

Arrange overlapping layers of potatoes in a casserole, dotting each layer with butter and sprinkling lightly with salt, white pepper, and some of the grated cheese. Repeat the layers, ending with cheese; be sure to reserve 1/4 cup cheese.

Bring the beef stock almost to a boil and gently pour over the potatoes. Bake 45 minutes, covering loosely with foil if the potatoes appear to be browning too quickly. When the potatoes are tender, remove from the oven.

To prepare the cream topping, beat the egg, sour cream, and heavy cream together, add the 1/4 cup grated cheese, and spread over the casserole. Return to the oven and bake until golden, about 5 minutes. Dust with parsley and serve.

Potato Latkes

SERVES 8

These are delicious with any meat dish, especially beef and lamb.

5 large potatoes
2 eggs, lightly beaten
2 tablespoons flour, or 1 tablespoon matzoh meal
1 teaspoon baking powder
1 teaspoon salt
Freshly ground pepper to taste
1 small onion, grated
Vegetable shortening for frying
Applesauce or sour cream (optional)

Peel the potatoes, grate on a fine grater, and squeeze out most of the liquid. Add the eggs to the potatoes. Add the dry ingredients and the onion and mix the batter well.

Melt the shortening in a skillet to a depth of about ½ inch, and drop the batter by tablespoons into the hot fat. Fry on both sides until brown, about 3 to 5 minutes; then drain on paper towels. Serve hot. If desired, serve applesauce or sour cream alongside.

Rice Pilaf

SERVES 4

This is especially good with any lamb dish.

3 tablespoons butter
3 tablespoons finely chopped onion
2 tablespoons finely chopped celery
1 cup long-grain rice
1 garlic clove, peeled
1 1/2 cups Chicken Stock (see recipe)
Salt and freshly ground pepper to taste
1 bay leaf
6 sprigs parsley
2 sprigs thyme, or 1/2 teaspoon dried
1 or 2 drops Tabasco sauce

Heat the butter in a saucepan over medium heat. When butter begins to sizzle, add the onion and celery and cook until tender, stirring constantly. Add the rice and garlic clove and cook, stirring, for a few minutes. Add the chicken stock, salt, pepper, bay leaf, parsley, thyme, and Tabasco to taste. Bring to a quick boil, reduce the heat to medium, cover the pot with a tight-fitting lid, and cook about 15 minutes, or until the rice is tender and all the liquid is absorbed.

Remove the garlic clove, bay leaf, and parsley and thyme sprigs and discard. Serve at once.

Salads and Salad Dressings

Dominique's is not a health-food restaurant, so we don't serve too many salads. Our Caesar salad is very popular, and the Green Bean Salad with Truffle Dressing created by our chefs is rich enough to enjoy as a main course. The most important thing to remember about salads is that all ingredients must be absolutely fresh. At the restaurants, we inspect the vegetables and lettuces very carefully. Old lettuce is like an old piece of fish; it will ruin the dish you're making, and no one will want you to cook for them again! Clean the lettuces carefully and store them in the refrigerator, loosely wrapped in paper towels. There is no economy in buying lots of lettuce at once, because if it spoils before you have a chance to eat it, the lettuce will have to be thrown away. Experiment with a variety of lettuces, greens, fresh herbs, oils, and vinegars. Unusual combinations will surprise you with new, fresh tastes, and even the diehard lettuce-loather may perk up at the taste of blueberry vinegar, delicate walnut oil, or watercress and dandelion greens.

Caesar Salad Dominique

SERVES 4

This salad is very popular at Dominique's.

The Caesar Oil and Garlic Croutons must be made ahead. The special oil can be stored for several weeks, and leftover oil is delicious when used to sauté eggplant slices, onions, or quail breasts.

2 garlic cloves, peeled
6 large anchovies, rinsed in cold water and chopped
2/3 cup Caesar Oil (see following recipe)
Juice of 1 lemon
Freshly ground black pepper
1 coddled egg (see Note)
1 large head romaine, cleaned and torn into pieces
1 cup freshly grated Parmesan or a blend of Parmesan and Romano
1 cup Garlic Croutons (see recipe)

Rub a large wooden bowl with the garlic cloves, then combine the anchovies, Caesar Oil, lemon juice, pepper, and egg in the bowl and blend well. Add the lettuce pieces and toss to coat thoroughly. Add ¾ cup cheese and toss again.

To serve, place in chilled individual salad bowls, top with croutons, and sprinkle with the remaining ¼ cup cheese.

NOTE: To coddle an egg, poach 1 minute, then drain on paper towel.

Caesar Oil

MAKES 1 CUP

1 cup good-quality olive oil
2 garlic cloves, peeled and finely chopped
1 anchovy, rinsed in cold water and finely chopped

Combine all the ingredients, cover tightly, and set aside at least 4 hours, so that the flavors can develop.

Garlic Croutons

MAKES ABOUT 1 CUP

4 slices 2-day-old French bread or other white bread
2 to 4 garlic cloves, peeled (depending on taste)

Toast the stale bread slices on both sides. While warm, rub with garlic cloves, cut into cubes, and let cool.

Dandelion Salad

SERVES 4

Dandelions should be picked in the early spring when quite young. Look for small leaves when buying them at the market; the darker leaves are tough and quite bitter in taste.

4 small handfuls young dandelion greens
¼ pound bacon
2 hard-boiled eggs, chopped
Salt and freshly ground pepper to taste
1½ tablespoons red wine vinegar
2 tablespoons chopped fresh parsley

Trim the roots of young dandelions and rinse three times in cold water. Drain and pat dry with paper towels. Chill in the refrigerator.

Fry the bacon until crisp, drain on paper towels, and reserve the fat.

To assemble the salad, place the chilled greens in a deep salad bowl. Top with the chopped eggs, salt, and pepper. Crumble the bacon, and sprinkle over the salad.

Reheat the reserved bacon fat, remove from the heat, and quickly stir in the vinegar. Pour over the salad, add parsley, and toss. Serve immediately on warmed salad plates.

Hot Romaine and Escarole Salad

SERVES 4 TO 6

1 tablespoon red wine vinegar
2 tablespoons fresh lemon juice
1 teaspoon sugar
1 tablespoon Dijon mustard
½ teaspoon Worcestershire sauce
2 garlic cloves, minced or pressed
6 strips of bacon, cut into ½-inch pieces
Vegetable or olive oil (optional)
1 medium onion, finely chopped
6 cups torn romaine leaves
4 cups torn escarole leaves
1 medium tomato, cut into thin wedges
Freshly ground pepper to taste

In a small bowl, combine the vinegar, lemon juice, sugar, mustard, Worcestershire, and garlic and blend well.

In a large skillet cook the bacon until crisp and brown, stirring often. Remove the bacon pieces with a slotted spoon and drain. Measure ¼ cup of the bacon drippings. Add oil if needed to make ¼ cup; discard any excess drippings. Return the drippings to the pan and cook the onion over medium heat, stirring, for about 1 minute. Mix in the lemon juice mixture and bring to a boil.

Place the romaine and escarole pieces in a large salad bowl with tomato wedges, and pour the hot dressing over. Toss to coat evenly. Sprinkle with the reserved bacon pieces and freshly ground pepper.

Green Bean Salad
with Truffle Dressing

SERVES 4

We serve this in Miami Beach as a separate course or as a main course at lunch.

1 pound small French green beans (haricots vert)
½ pound large white mushrooms
Juice of 1 lemon
½ teaspoon chopped shallots
1 teaspoon chopped truffle
1 egg yolk
½ cup vegetable oil
¼ cup walnut oil
¼ cup sherry vinegar
¼ cup truffle juice
Salt and freshly ground pepper to taste
4 large radicchio leaves, rinsed and dried, for garnish
3 Belgian endives, separated into leaves, for garnish
1 tablespoon chopped fresh herbs, such as parsley, chives, and tarragon,
for garnish

Trim the ends of the green beans and remove the strings (if any). Place in a pot of boiling water and cook 8 minutes, or until tender but still crisp. Drain in a colander, refresh under cold running water, and reserve.

Wipe the mushrooms with damp paper towels, trim, and discard the stems. Slice into strips approximately the same width as the green beans. Sprinkle with lemon juice, and set aside.

In a large bowl combine the shallots, truffle, and egg yolk. Stir with a whisk and gradually add the vegetable oil, whisking constantly; then whisk in the walnut oil, sherry vinegar, truffle juice, and salt and pepper.

Combine the green beans and mushrooms, add the dressing, and toss gently to coat. Arrange the radicchio and endive leaves on a large round platter. Place the green bean salad in the center, and sprinkle with chopped fresh herbs.

Creamy Coleslaw

SERVES 4 TO 6

Serve this tasty cabbage salad as a garniture with cold meat platters, smoked poultry, and luncheon dishes.

3/4 cup mayonnaise
1/3 cup sour cream
1 teaspoon salt
1 teaspoon celery seed
1 teaspoon prepared mustard
1 dash of freshly ground pepper
1 tablespoon sugar
1 tablespoon white vinegar
1 to 1 1/2 pounds green cabbage, shredded (about 8 to 9 cups)
4 scallions, thinly sliced
2 tablespoons chopped fresh parsley for garnish

Blend the mayonnaise, sour cream, salt, celery seed, mustard, pepper, sugar, and vinegar thoroughly. In a large bowl, combine the shredded cabbage and scallions, add the dressing, and toss to coat evenly. Cover and refrigerate for at least 4 hours or overnight. The coleslaw improves with aging.

To serve, toss gently and sprinkle with parsley.

French Potato Salad

SERVES 4

Always dress a potato salad while the potatoes are hot, so they can absorb the dressing and flavors. It is best eaten cold or at room temperature. To dress this up, you can serve it on shredded lettuce or Belgian endive leaves, garnished with capers or anchovy fillets.

1 pound new potatoes, scrubbed
Vinaigrette Dressing (see following recipe)
4 tablespoons grated onion
4 tablespoons chopped fresh parsley

Boil the new potatoes in their skins until tender. Remove the skins and dice while still warm. Add the vinaigrette, toss, then add the onions and parsley. Chill or serve at room temperature.

Vinaigrette Dressing

MAKES ABOUT 3/4 CUP

1 teaspoon Dijon mustard
Salt and freshly ground pepper to taste
6 tablespoons olive or vegetable oil
3 tablespoons wine vinegar or white vinegar
1 garlic clove, crushed
2 tablespoons chopped fresh chives or tarragon

Combine all the ingredients in a bowl, beating with a heavy whisk, or process in a blender or food processor.

Mélange of
Fresh Vegetables Vinaigrette

SERVES 4

Try this Miami Beach creation with young, fresh vegetables.

2 carrots, peeled
2 medium zucchini
1 small head cauliflower
1 stalk broccoli
5 ounces fresh snow peas
5 ounces string beans
¼ cup lemon juice
Dominique's Vinaigrette (see recipe)
Salt and freshly ground pepper to taste (optional)

Bring a large pot of salted water to a boil. While the water is heating, prepare the vegetables, keeping each vegetable separate.

Cut the carrots into julienne strips about 2 inches long, and set aside. Cut the zucchini into julienne strips about 2 inches long, and set aside. Separate the cauliflower into florets, discard the stems, and set aside. Separate the broccoli into florets, discarding the stem, and set aside. Wash and string the snow peas, and set aside. Wash the string beans, remove strings (if any) and set aside.

When the water boils, plunge the broccoli into the pot and cook until tender but still crisp. Remove and refresh under cold running water, drain, and place in a large bowl. Do the same with the snow peas, then the string beans, carrots, and zucchini. Add the lemon juice to the water and cook the cauliflower until tender but still crisp; refresh under cold water, drain, and add to other vegetables. Pour Dominique's Vinaigrette over the vegetables, toss gently, and taste and adjust the seasoning with salt and pepper, if necessary.

Tarragon Chicken Salad

SERVES 8 TO 10

4 pounds boneless chicken breasts, skin removed
Salt and freshly ground pepper to taste
1 1/2 cups Crème Fraîche (see recipe)
3/4 cup sour cream
3/4 cup mayonnaise
1 cup finely chopped celery leaves
1/2 cup finely chopped fresh parsley
3/4 cup whole walnut or pecan pieces
6 tablespoons chopped fresh tarragon, or 2 tablespoons dried
Juice of 1 lemon
1 cup pitted Greek olives

Preheat the oven to 375°F.

Cut the chicken breasts in thick slices. Dust with salt and pepper. Arrange the chicken in a large baking dish. Spread the crème fraîche on top. Cover and bake about 35 minutes, or until done. Let the chicken cool, and cut into cubes.

Combine the sour cream, mayonnaise, celery leaves, parsley, walnuts or pecans, tarragon, lemon juice, and olives. Add the mixture to the chicken meat, tossing to combine. Cover and refrigerate overnight. Taste and adjust the seasoning before serving.

Smoked Bluefish Salad

SERVES 4

We serve this in Washington, D.C., in the summer when bluefish are plentiful. I used to smoke the bluefish on my farm in Maryland, but I'm happier with the consistency of the fish that is smoked by the suppliers we now use. This can be served as an appetizer, or made into sandwiches for a special treat.

1 1/2 pounds smoked bluefish, all skin and bones discarded
2/3 cup mayonnaise
1 large tart apple
3 celery stalks, diced
3 scallions, including the green tops, thinly sliced
Juice of 1/2 lemon
White pepper to taste
Lettuce leaves

Cut the bluefish into 1-inch chunks, and toss with the mayonnaise. Core the apple and dice, leaving the skin on, and add to the bluefish. Add all remaining ingredients except lettuce leaves, and toss to combine thoroughly. Serve on a bed of fresh crisp lettuce.

Smoked Shellfish and Pasta Salad

SERVES 4 TO 6

This is a good main course, hearty and very flavorful.

1/2 pound pasta shells
1/4 pound cooked shrimp, peeled and left whole
1/4 pound smoked scallops, sliced
1/4 pound whole smoked mussels
10 marinated black Greek olives, pitted and coarsely chopped
3 ounces red wine vinegar
Juice of 1 lemon
1 large cooked carrot, sliced diagonally
2 scallions, including the green tops, sliced diagonally
4 tablespoons cooked green peas
1 1/2 cups extra-virgin olive oil
2 medium garlic cloves, finely minced
5 to 6 large white mushrooms, thinly sliced
Sour cream for garnish (optional)

Cook the pasta shells according to package directions, until *al dente*. Drain and place in a large bowl. Add all the remaining ingredients except sour cream, toss, and let sit at room temperature for at least 1 hour to allow the flavors to develop. Toss before serving. Garnish with a dollop of sour cream, if desired.

Rattlesnake Salad

SERVES 4

Very popular in both Dominique's! Rattlesnake can be ordered from specialty food stores.

4 pounds rattlesnake, skinned and cleaned, head and tail removed
2 cups dry white wine
2 cups water
1 bouquet garni (see p. 32)
Salt and freshly ground pepper to taste
1/2 cup diced celery
1/3 cup diced Spanish onion
Juice of 1 lemon
1 tablespoon Dijon mustard
1/4 cup chopped fresh parsley
Mayonnaise
Lettuce leaves for garnish
Radishes for garnish

Cut the snake into pieces about 12 inches long. Place in a saucepan and cover with the white wine and water. Add the bouquet garni, salt, and pepper. Cover and bring to a boil, then reduce heat and simmer about 15 minutes, or until the meat is tender.

Remove the snake from the pan. When the meat is cool, remove it from the bones. Place the meat in a round bowl and add the celery, onion, lemon juice, mustard, salt and pepper to taste, and parsley. Gradually blend in enough mayonnaise to duplicate the consistency of your favorite tuna fish salad.

Serve on a bed of lettuce, garnished with fresh radishes.

Dominique's Vinaigrette

MAKES ABOUT 1 CUP

1 1/2 tablespoons Dijon mustard
4 tablespoons red wine vinegar
1 pinch of sugar
Salt and freshly ground pepper to taste
2 tablespoons finely chopped fresh parsley, celery leaves, or chives, or 1
*   tablespoon chopped fresh tarragon*
1/2 cup good-quality olive oil

Place the mustard in a salad bowl and whisk in the vinegar, sugar, salt, pepper, and fresh herbs of your choice. Add the oil gradually, beating constantly with the whisk. Taste and adjust the seasoning.

Basil Dressing

MAKES ABOUT 1/3 CUP

2 tablespoons vegetable oil
2 tablespoons olive oil
2 tablespoons red wine vinegar
1 garlic clove, minced or pressed
1/2 teaspoon sugar
1/2 teaspoon salt
1/3 cup lightly packed fresh basil leaves, rinsed well and coarsely chopped
Freshly ground pepper to taste

In a blender, combine all the ingredients and whirl until very well blended. Taste and adjust the seasoning.

Dominique's
Blue Cheese Dressing

MAKES 2 1/2 CUPS

Make ahead and refrigerate overnight to get the full flavor of the cheese and herbs in this dressing.

³/₄ cup sour cream
¹/₂ teaspoon dry mustard
¹/₂ teaspoon freshly ground pepper
1 pinch of salt
1 garlic clove, minced
1 teaspoon Worcestershire sauce
2 tablespoons minced fresh chives or parsley
1 ¹/₃ cups mayonnaise
4 ounces imported Danish blue cheese, crumbled

Combine all the ingredients except the mayonnaise and cheese, stirring to blend well. Gently fold in the mayonnaise and blue cheese, cover, and refrigerate overnight.

Creamy Lemon Dressing

MAKES 1 QUART

2 eggs
2 garlic cloves, crushed and finely chopped
Salt and freshly ground pepper to taste
3 cups vegetable oil
1 tablespoon Worcestershire sauce
¹/₂ cup freshly squeezed lemon juice
4 tablespoons finely chopped chives

In a chilled round-bottomed glass bowl, beat the eggs with a wire whisk. Add the garlic, salt, and pepper and stir to combine. Slowly add the oil, whisking constantly, until the dressing thickens. Add the Worcestershire and lemon juice, beating well to combine. Taste and adjust the seasoning. Stir in the chives. Chill in the refrigerator, covered, in a glass jar. Shake well before using.

Creole Roquefort Dressing

MAKES ABOUT 1 CUP

2 small garlic cloves, finely chopped
¼ cup white wine vinegar
1 tablespoon fresh lemon juice
4 anchovy fillets, rinsed in cold water and drained
2½ teaspoons minced fresh oregano, or 1 teaspoon dried
1 teaspoon celery salt
¼ teaspoon salt
1 egg
¼ cup coarsely crumbled Roquefort cheese or other blue cheese (1 ounce)
½ teaspoon Dijon mustard
½ teaspoon sugar
¾ cup good-quality olive oil

In the work bowl of a food processor fitted with a steel blade, or in a blender with the motor running, drop garlic through feed tube to mince. Add all the ingredients except the olive oil. Process until blended, about 5 seconds. Stop the machine and scrape down the sides of the bowl. With the motor running, pour the oil through feed tube in a slow, steady stream. Process until combined. Pour into a bowl; cover and refrigerate until chilled, or up to 3 days before serving. Whisk briefly before using on vegetable salads or dark greens, such as spinach.

Sauces and Gravies

Emulsified sauces are the current favorite from French classic cuisine. In search of lightness, more and more chefs all over the world have turned away from traditional flour-based sauces to the delicate emulsions whose principal ingredient is butter. Flavor and texture is the main characteristic of all sauces. A touch too much seasoning, a little too much heat, and the sauce is gone forever.

Another useful way to thicken sauces is by using beurre manié, a mixture of butter and flour that is added to the sauce at the end of cooking, rather than at the beginning. Cream the butter, and work in an equal quantity of flour with a fork or whisk. To use, drop pieces of beurre manié into the boiling sauce, whisking hard. The butter will melt and distribute the flour evenly through the liquid. Keep adding pieces of beurre manié until the sauce is thick enough to coat a spoon or to please you, then simmer the sauce for at least 5 minutes to cook the flour, eliminating the raw-flour taste.

There are an unlimited number of French sauces that I could list in this book; we use quite a few in both restaurants.

I've included many sauces on the same pages as the meats or fish they accompany. However, in this chapter I'm giving you the best of the best—a good selection of sauces to dress up *all* your meals.

Clarified Butter

MAKES 3/4 TO 1 CUP

While not strictly a sauce, clarified butter will improve all your cooking. Clarified butter is butter with all the impurities removed. It will not burn as easily as unclarified butter, and should always be used when sautéing meat, fish, or vegetables.

Clarified butter can be kept safely, covered, in the refrigerator for about 3 weeks.

To prepare, cut ½ pound unsalted butter into small pieces. Melt over low heat. As soon as the butter melts, remove it from the heat and let rest 1 or 2 minutes. Skim the foam and residue from the top. Pour the golden yellow butter into a clean container, leaving behind the milky residue that has settled to the bottom of the pan.

Demi-glace or Brown Sauce

MAKES ABOUT 2 1/2 CUPS

This is basic to every kitchen. It keeps indefinitely in the freezer, so you can always have some on hand. For storage suggestions see p. 32.

5 pounds meaty veal bones, chopped into 3- or 4-inch pieces
1 cup coarsely chopped carrots
2 cups coarsely chopped onions
1 cup coarsely chopped celery
8 peppercorns
2 bay leaves
3 garlic cloves, unpeeled, cut in half
4 sprigs thyme, or 1 teaspoon dried
16 cups water
1 cup loosely packed parsley or celery leaves
3 cups coarsely chopped tomatoes

Preheat the oven to 400°F.

Put the bones in a large flat roasting pan. Place in the oven and bake 2½ hours, stirring and turning the bones every 45 minutes. Then, layer the carrots, onions, celery, peppercorns, bay leaves, garlic, and thyme over the roasted bones. Bake 30 minutes longer, stirring from time to time.

Transfer the contents of roasting pan to a large kettle. Add 2 cups water to the roasting pan and stir to dissolve the brown particles that cling to the bottom and sides of the pan. Add this to the kettle. Add the remaining 14 cups water to the kettle. Add the parsley or celery leaves and tomatoes. Bring to a boil, reduce heat, and simmer slowly over very low heat for about 12 to 14 hours. (The best demi-glace simmers very slowly, taking the maximum cooking time. Skim the surface often during the first 3 hours. Then let it simmer undisturbed, overnight.)

Strain the liquid through cheesecloth, discarding the solids. Cool to room temperature and store in jars or plastic containers. This stock will keep for weeks in the refrigerator and indefinitely in the freezer.

Meat or Fish Glaze

MAKES 1 CUP

Boil 3 quarts Demi-glace or Fish Stock (see recipes) until reduced to about 1 cup. As the stock reduces, transfer it to smaller saucepans and lower the heat progressively to a slow simmer to avoid scorching. The finished glaze will be dark and syrupy and will set very firmly when it cools. Glaze can be kept, tightly covered and refrigerated, for several months. Meat or fish glaze is used in very small quantities to add body to sauces and ragouts.

Marinade for Chicken, Beef, or Lamb

MAKES 1 1/2 CUPS

1/2 cup olive oil
1/2 cup dry white wine
2 tablespoons red wine vinegar
2 tablespoons lemon juice
2 garlic cloves, pressed
2 tablespoons Dijon mustard
1 pinch of sugar
1 pinch of salt
1 pinch of dried oregano
1 pinch of dried tarragon
1 pinch of dried thyme
1/4 teaspoon white pepper

Combine all the ingredients in a blender. If fresh herbs are available, use them instead of dried.

Easy Sauce for Wild Fowl

MAKES 1 CUP

Good for any game bird, braised or roasted.

2 cups Chicken Stock (see recipe)
⅓ cup diced onion
8 whole peppercorns
6 sprigs parsley, chopped
½ cup diced celery
1 bay leaf
3 tablespoons unsalted butter, at room temperature
3 tablespoons all-purpose flour
¾ cup dry white wine
1 cup heavy cream
Salt and freshly ground white pepper to taste
3 tablespoons Cognac
4 tablespoons chopped fresh parsley

Place the chicken stock in a saucepan and add the diced onions, peppercorns, chopped parsley sprigs, celery, and bay leaf. Bring to a quick boil and reduce to 1 cup. Remove from the heat and set aside.

Blend the butter and flour into a smooth paste (beurre manié; see p. 90). Add, bit by bit, to the chicken stock, blending well with a whisk. Return the saucepan to the heat and simmer slowly 5 minutes. Add the wine and cook over medium heat 5 minutes more, stirring constantly to prevent scorching. Remove from the heat and add the cream. Return to the heat and simmer 2 minutes more.

Strain the sauce, discarding the solids. Add the salt and white pepper, and blend in the Cognac and 4 tablespoons chopped parsley (for color). Serve warm.

Barbecue Sauce

MAKES 2 CUPS

This flavorful sauce is just right for marinating or basting meat, fish, or poultry. Try it with Oven-Barbecued Alligator (see recipe) for a tasty variation.

8 ounces tomato sauce
1 teaspoon dried mustard
1 teaspoon sugar
1 teaspoon salt
1 tablespoon Worcestershire sauce
1 tablespoon red wine vinegar
1/2 cup dry red wine
1 cup chopped onion
2 garlic cloves, chopped
1 bay leaf
3 drops Tabasco sauce
1/2 cup olive oil for basting

Blend all the ingredients except the olive oil in a saucepan. Bring to a boil, then reduce the heat and simmer 10 minutes. Strain, and use to marinate meat. For basting, add the olive oil to the marinade.

Quick Chicken Gravy

MAKES 1 1/2 CUPS

A recipe to make when you roast a chicken.

2 tablespoons chicken fat (from roasting pan)
1 cup Chicken Stock (see recipe)
1 teaspoon arrowroot, dissolved in 2 tablespoons water
Salt and freshly ground pepper to taste
1/3 cup coarsely chopped fresh parsley
1 garlic clove, mashed

Once the chicken is roasted, remove it from the roasting pan and keep warm. Skim all but 2 tablespoons chicken fat from the pan juices. Add the chicken stock to the roasting pan and scrape up all the solids clinging to the bottom and sides. Deglaze, then strain the liquid through a fine sieve into a small saucepan. Add the dissolved arrowroot and stir well. Add salt and pepper and any chicken juice that has accumulated on the platter. Stir in the parsley and garlic, bring to a boil, and simmer 5 minutes. Remove the garlic clove, and serve the gravy with the roasted chicken.

Spanish Creole Sauce

MAKES 2 CUPS

We use this sauce in both restaurants. In Miami Beach, where we offer brunch, it's served with egg dishes, and we've just begun serving it with catfish. You can serve this chunky sauce with omelets, hot rice, chicken, or fish.

2 onions, thinly sliced
2 green peppers, seeded and finely chopped
3 tablespoons olive oil
5 large ripe tomatoes, peeled and seeded (about 2 cups)
1/4 teaspoon salt
1/2 teaspoon paprika, or 1 drop of Tabasco sauce
1 teaspoon fresh lemon juice
4 tablespoons chopped fresh parsley

Sauté the onions and peppers in the olive oil. Add the tomatoes, season with salt and paprika or Tabasco, and cook slowly until the vegetables are tender. Add the lemon juice and parsley.

Madeira Sauce

MAKES 1 CUP

This sauce is a classic accompaniment to fillet of beef, veal, ham, tongue, and Kidney Sauté with Madeira.

1 cup Demi-glace or Brown Sauce (see recipe)
3 tablespoons Madeira
Salt and freshly ground pepper to taste (optional)

Heat the demi-glace in a saucepan, add 1½ tablespoons Madeira, and simmer 10 minutes. Add the remaining 1½ tablespoons Madeira and bring just to a boil. Taste for seasoning, and add salt and pepper if necessary.

Green Peppercorn Sauce for Fowl

MAKES 3 CUPS

⅓ cup dry white wine
2 tablespoons brandy
2 tablespoons green peppercorns, drained
2 cups Chicken Stock (see recipe) or stock from wild birds, if available
1 cup light cream
1 teaspoon red wine vinegar
2 tablespoons chopped fresh parsley
Salt and freshly ground pepper to taste (optional)

In a saucepan, combine the wine and brandy. Simmer to reduce by half. Add the peppercorns and boil 1 minute. Add the stock and simmer 10 minutes. Stir in the cream, reduce heat, and simmer gently 5 minutes. Add the vinegar and parsley and stir well. Taste and adjust the seasoning with salt and pepper, if necessary. Serve with roasted or baked fowl.

Porto Sauce
for Duck or Chicken

MAKES ABOUT 1 QUART

You can make this sauce ahead and store it in the refrigerator. Reheat in the top of a double boiler.

1/2 cup raisins
2 cups good-quality port
2 cups Chicken Stock (see recipe)
1 cup red currant jelly
2 2/3 tablespoons cornstarch
1 1/2 teaspoons grated fresh ginger
1/4 teaspoon white pepper

In a small bowl, let the raisins macerate in the port for 12 hours or overnight.

In a large saucepan, whisk together all the ingredients. Bring to a boil, stirring constantly, and reduce sauce to 1 quart. Taste and adjust the seasonings, and serve with roasted duck or chicken.

Ravigote Sauce

MAKES ABOUT 2 1/2 CUPS

A classic sauce, ravigote is good served with fish, such as mackerel, chicken, brains, and even eggs.

1/2 cup dry white wine
1/4 cup red wine vinegar
5 tablespoons butter
4 tablespoons all-purpose flour
2 cups Beef Stock or Chicken Stock (see recipes)
2 shallots, minced
2 tablespoons minced fresh chervil
2 tablespoons minced fresh tarragon
1 tablespoon chopped fresh chives
Salt and freshly ground pepper to taste

Combine the wine and vinegar in a saucepan and simmer to reduce by half. Set aside.

Melt the butter in a skillet and blend in the flour, but do not brown. Add the stock and cook until thickened, stirring constantly. Add the thickened stock to the wine mixture and simmer 5 minutes. Add the shallots and herbs, and season to taste.

Tomato Sauce with Cream

MAKES 2 QUARTS

Serve with your favorite pasta, or mix with steamed vegetables, top with grated Swiss cheese or Parmesan, and bake until the cheese is golden brown.

3 tablespoons olive oil
1 carrot, finely chopped
1 Spanish onion, finely chopped
2 celery stalks with leaves, finely chopped
3 garlic cloves, mashed
3 tablespoons tomato paste
16 ripe tomatoes, peeled, seeded, and chopped
2 quarts Chicken Stock (see recipe)
1/3 cup coarsely chopped fresh basil
1 bouquet garni (see p. 32)
1 bay leaf
1/2 cup heavy cream
6 tablespoons butter, cut into small pieces
1 tablespoon salt
Freshly ground pepper to taste

In a large skillet, heat the olive oil to sizzling. Add the carrot, onion, and celery, and sauté until tender, about 8 minutes. Add the garlic and cook 2 minutes more. Stir in the tomato paste, tomatoes, chicken stock, basil, bouquet garni, and bay leaf. Bring to a boil, reduce heat, and simmer 1 hour. Remove the bouquet garni and bay leaf and discard.

Place the sauce in a food processor or blender and purée until smooth. Strain through a fine sieve. Reduce over medium heat until the sauce thickens. Add the cream, then gradually whisk in the butter, a few pieces at a time, stirring well after each addition. Add the salt and pepper.

Red Wine Sauce with Thyme

MAKES ABOUT 1 CUP

1 small sprig thyme
2 cups dry red wine
4 tablespoons finely chopped shallots, or 6 tablespoons finely chopped onion
Salt and freshly ground pepper to taste
1 cup (2 sticks) very cold unsalted butter, cut into 6 pieces
1/2 teaspoon sugar
Juice of 1/2 lemon
1 teaspoon Cognac or brandy

Combine the thyme, wine, and shallots or onions in a saucepan.
Bring to a boil and simmer gently until reduced to 3/4 cup.
Remove the thyme and discard. Continue simmering gently
until reduced to 1/4 cup. Add salt and pepper to taste. Remove
from the heat and whisk in the butter, 1 piece at a time. Add the
sugar, lemon juice, and Cognac. Serve immediately with meat or
fish, or keep warm in the top of a double boiler over warm water
until ready to use.

Meats

Washington, D.C., with its open spaces and river views, is perhaps the most beautiful, the most pleasant city in America. Add to this the tremendous power that radiates from the White House, from Capitol Hill, and from the embassies, and it is easy to understand why Washingtonians love their city and why millions of people visit here each year.

At the end of the day, with tired feet and weary minds, these people come to Dominique's restaurant (without reservations), ask for the best-located table, and then complain if they must wait in line. In any case, once their meal arrives, these guests realize what great dining is all about—namely, the finest and freshest ingredients prepared with skill and imagination by master chefs.

Because our dinner menu is as thick as a bible, our guests generally prefer to receive our suggestions. The following group of recipes, along with others in this volume, are those that we recommend to our most demanding customers. Many of these recipes have been requested often and have been mailed to patrons all over the world. I include them here so that you can enjoy them in your own home—including our most popular menu item of all, Roasted Racks of Lamb Dominique. Prepare these recipes for your family and guests, and you will have the great satisfaction of knowing that you are offering the very best at your table.

Brisket of Beef
with Mustard Sauce

SERVES 4 TO 6

This is one of Dominique's specials that we serve at lunch—a good, hearty meal to help you get through a busy afternoon. It's a wonderful dish for dinner, served with potatoes, a salad, and a good red wine.

2 pounds lean brisket of beef
Salt and freshly ground pepper to taste
1 small Spanish onion, finely chopped
3 celery stalks, thinly sliced
1 red pepper, seeded and cut into ¹/₂-inch dice
8 sprigs parsley
1 bay leaf
¹/₂ cup dry white wine
1 tablespoon dry mustard, dissolved in 3 tablespoons cold water for 15
    minutes
¹/₂ cup sour cream
1 teaspoon red wine vinegar
4 tablespoons chopped fresh parsley

Preheat the oven to 350°F.
    Rinse the meat with cold water and pat dry with paper towels. Sprinkle with salt and pepper. Place the onion, celery,

red pepper, parsley sprigs, and bay leaf in the bottom of a buttered casserole. Pour the wine over, then lay the meat on top. Cover and bake about 3 hours, or until the brisket is tender.

Combine the dissolved dry mustard with the sour cream and vinegar, and set aside.

Slice the meat thinly and arrange on a warm ovenproof platter. Pour the sauce over the meat and return to the oven for 5 minutes. Dust with chopped parsley. Serve with mashed or boiled potatoes.

Brisket of Beef with Sweet Potato and Prune Tzimmes

SERVES 6 TO 8

1 ½ pounds prunes
3 cups boiling water
2 teaspoons chicken fat
3 pounds boneless chuck or brisket (see Note)
1 onion, chopped
1 ½ teaspoons salt
¼ teaspoon pepper
5 medium sweet potatoes, peeled and coarsely chopped
⅓ cup brown sugar, or ½ cup honey
½ teaspoon cinnamon

Wash the prunes, place in a large bowl, and pour the boiling water over. Set aside. Melt the chicken fat in a Dutch oven or large heavy saucepan. Cut the beef into 8 pieces, and brown with the onion in the fat. Sprinkle with salt and pepper, cover, and cook over low heat for 1 hour.

Add the prunes and their soaking liquid, the sweet potatoes, sugar or honey, and cinnamon. Replace the cover loosely and cook over low heat about 2 hours, or place it in a casserole and bake in a preheated 350°F. oven until the meat is tender, about 45 minutes.

NOTE: You may substitute other combinations of meat, such as chicken breasts or lamb chops, with fruits or fresh vegetables, or just a good combination of fresh fruits alone for this recipe. To ensure the best taste, it is important that this dish be cooked slowly for the best blending of flavors.

Fillets of Beef "en Chemise" with Green Peppercorn Sauce

SERVES 4

An elegant creation of our Miami Beach kitchen.

CRÊPE BATTER

⅓ cup all-purpose flour
1 teaspoon sugar
1 pinch of salt
2 eggs
1 cup milk
1 tablespoon butter, melted and cooled
Butter for skillet

FILLETS AND SAUCE

Salt and freshly ground pepper to taste
4 center-cut filet mignon steaks (6 ounces each)
4 tablespoons unsalted butter
Juice from 1 can green peppercorns
4 teaspoons green peppercorns
2 tablespoons Cognac or brandy
2 tablespoons good-quality port
2 tablespoons red wine
2 tablespoons dry white wine
½ cup Demi-glace or Brown Sauce (see recipe)
1 cup heavy cream
1 red pepper, seeded and finely diced
4 teaspoons chopped fresh parsley for garnish

To prepare the crêpes, combine the flour, sugar, salt, and eggs. Whisk in the milk until the batter is smooth. Add the cooled butter and stir to blend. Cover the bowl and refrigerate for at least 1 hour. Lightly butter a crêpe pan or skillet measuring 6½ to 7 inches across the bottom. Pour a scant ¼ cup of batter into the middle, and tilt the pan quickly in all directions to spread the batter thinly over the entire bottom of the pan. Set on medium-high heat and cook about 1 minute. Lift the edges of the crêpe with a spatula and, if the underside is light brown, turn and cook on other side for 30 seconds. Remove the crêpe to a warm plate and cover with a bowl to keep warm. Do not regrease the pan. Continue making crêpes until all the batter is used.

To prepare the fillets, salt and pepper the filets mignons. Melt 1 tablespoon butter in a skillet and cook the meat over high heat 5 to 7 minutes on each side for rare meat. For meat cooked medium-well, continue cooking a few minutes longer, but do not overcook. Remove the fillets to an ovenproof plate and keep warm in a very low oven while you prepare the sauce.

Deglaze the skillet with the green peppercorn juice and green peppercorns, stirring well to dissolve any particles clinging to the bottom of the pan. Add the Cognac, port, and red and white wines and reduce. Add the demi-glace and continue boiling to reduce by half. Add the heavy cream and reduce until the sauce has a thick, smooth consistency (and coats the back of a spoon). Whisk in the remaining 3 tablespoons butter, remove from the heat, and add the diced red pepper.

To assemble, place each filet mignon in the center of a crêpe, fold it to enclose the meat, and place on a dinner plate. Spoon the sauce over, and sprinkle with chopped parsley. Serve immediately.

NOTE: If you have any leftover crêpes, stack them with plastic wrap between each crêpe, wrap tightly, and freeze for later use.

Steak au Poivre

SERVES 4

This classic French dish is very popular at Dominique's.

4 prime center-cut sirloin steaks (14 ounces each)
4 tablespoons cracked black peppercorns
Salt to taste
4 tablespoons vegetable oil
2 tablespoons lemon juice
8 tablespoons butter
2 garlic cloves, crushed and chopped
3 tablespoons chopped shallots
1/2 cup red wine
2 tablespoons chopped fresh parsley
Freshly ground pepper to taste

The steaks should be cut from the center of a New York strip. Press the cracked peppercorns firmly against both sides of each steak. Sprinkle both sides with salt. Combine 2 tablespoons vegetable oil with 1 tablespoon lemon juice, and brush gently over the steaks.

Heat the remaining 2 tablespoons vegetable oil in a large skillet and brown the steaks over moderate heat for 5 minutes on each side for medium-rare meat. Remove the steaks to an ovenproof platter and keep warm in a very low oven. Pour out the oil and discard.

Add 2 tablespoons butter to the skillet and sauté the garlic and shallots until tender. Add the wine and bring to a boil, reduce the heat, and simmer until reduced to one-third. Remove from the heat and stir in remaining 6 tablespoons butter, 1 tablespoon at a time, and the remaining lemon juice and parsley. Add salt and pepper to taste. Place the skillet over high heat and bring to a simmer. Pour the sauce over the steaks or pass separately in a sauceboat. Serve with potatoes of your choice.

Calf's Head Vinaigrette

SERVES 4 TO 8

A very popular dish in Washington, D.C., where we serve it with Sauce Gribiche and boiled potatoes.

½ calf's head
1 large onion, finely chopped
2 carrots, finely chopped
Juice of 2 lemons
6 peppercorns
2 tablespoons all-purpose flour
2 whole cloves
1 bouquet garni (see p. 32)
Salt to taste
Sauce Gribiche (see following recipe)
1 cup chopped fresh parsley for garnish
Lemon wedges for garnish

Have your butcher clean and bone the calf's head. Fill a deep pot with enough water to cover the meat entirely. Place the chopped onion, carrots, lemon juice, peppercorns, flour, cloves, bouquet garni, and salt in the pot. Bring to a boil and cook about 10 minutes. Add the calf's head, lower the heat, and simmer gently for 1 hour and 35 minutes, or until the meat is tender.

Remove the meat to a platter and let cool to room temperature. Slice, and serve with Sauce Gribiche. Garnish with lots of chopped parsley and lemon wedges.

NOTE: A well-seasoned vinaigrette may be used instead of Sauce Gribiche.

Sauce Gribiche

MAKES 3 CUPS

4 hard-boiled eggs
1 1/2 teaspoons Dijon mustard
Salt and freshly ground pepper to taste
2 cups olive oil
3/4 cup red wine vinegar
3/4 cup minced cornichons
1 teaspoon dried tarragon
2 teaspoons chopped fresh parsley

Separate the yolks from the whites. Mash the yolks in a round bowl. Add the mustard, salt, pepper, olive oil, vinegar, cornichons, tarragon, and parsley, and blend well. Dice the egg white in small pieces, and add to sauce. Chill.

Calf's Liver, Italian Style

SERVES 4

This is one of our daily specials on the restaurant menu, and it's always popular. We serve it with mashed potatoes.

3 tablespoons butter
2 tablespoons oil
2 medium Spanish onions, thinly sliced
1/4 teaspoon powdered sage
1 pound calf's liver, cleaned of all membranes and nerves
Salt and freshly ground pepper to taste
1/2 cup sifted all-purpose flour
Juice of 1 lemon
1/3 cup dry white wine
1 teaspoon red wine vinegar
2 tablespoons chopped fresh parsley

Melt 1½ tablespoons butter and 1 tablespoon oil in a heavy skillet, and add the onions. Sprinkle the sage over the onions, stir, cover, and simmer over low heat 10 to 15 minutes, or until the onions turn golden. Remove from the skillet and set aside.

Pat the liver dry with paper towels, and cut into ¼-inch strips about 4 inches long. Put the strips in a paper or plastic bag with salt, pepper, and flour. Hold the bag firmly closed and shake, tossing the meat to coat evenly with seasoned flour.

Add the remaining 1½ tablespoons butter and 1 tablespoon oil to the skillet and heat until very hot and sizzling. Shake the excess flour off the strips of meat, then place them in the skillet. Turn the meat to sear on both sides. Once the meat is browned, add the cooked onions, lemon juice, wine, and vinegar. Cover and simmer 1 to 2 minutes. Stir in the parsley, taste and adjust the seasoning, and serve at once.

Veal Chops Sauté Normande

SERVES 4

The combination of Calvados and cream makes this dish a unique and tasty entrée.

4 veal chops (1 inch thick), trimmed of all fat
¼ cup all-purpose flour, seasoned with ¼ teaspoon salt and ⅛ teaspoon
    pepper
1 tablespoon vegetable oil
2 tablespoons Clarified Butter (see recipe)
2 tablespoons Calvados or applejack
¾ cup White Veal Stock or Chicken Stock (see recipes)
½ cup heavy cream
Salt and freshly ground pepper to taste
1 tablespoon chopped fresh parsley or chives

Coat the chops lightly with seasoned flour and shake off the excess. In a sauté pan, heat the oil over medium heat and add the butter. Sauté the chops until well-browned, about 3 minutes on each side. Remove the pan from the heat, pour Calvados over the chops, and flame. When the alcohol is burned off, add the stock, cover, and simmer until the chops are tender, about 15 minutes. Remove the chops to a platter and keep warm.

Add the cream to the liquid in the sauté pan and reduce until the sauce is thick enough to coat the back of a spoon. Add salt and pepper. Pour the sauce over the chops and sprinkle with parsley or chives. Serve with Mushrooms Bordelaise (see recipe) or other mushrooms of your choice.

Veal Medaillions with Morel Sauce

SERVES 4

This creation of our chef in Miami Beach is a special recommendation of my assistant, Diana Damewood.

2 ounces dried morels, or 6 ounces fresh
1 1/2 pounds veal loin, cut into four 6-ounce medaillions
1 teaspoon salt
Freshly ground pepper to taste
1 tablespoon all-purpose flour
About 3 to 4 tablespoons unsalted butter
1 tablespoon oil, or more as needed
3 shallots, chopped
1/2 cup port
3/4 cup dry white wine
1 cup heavy cream
1/3 cup Demi-glace or Brown Sauce (see recipe)

If dried morels are used, soak them in 2 quarts warm water for 3 hours; if fresh morels are used, rinse well and trim off the stems.

Season the veal medaillions with salt and pepper, and dust lightly with flour. In a heavy skillet, heat 1 tablespoon butter and the oil. Sauté the medaillions until golden brown but still pink inside, about 3 to 4 minutes on each side. Add more butter and oil to skillet, if necessary. Transfer the veal to a warm platter and keep warm.

Pour off all but 1 tablespoon of the fat. Add the morels and chopped shallots and sauté 2 to 3 minutes. Remove the morels, and deglaze the pan with port and white wine. Reduce to ½ cup. Add the cream and continue to reduce over medium heat until the sauce is slightly thickened. Stir in the demi-glace and remove from the heat. Slowly whisk in 1½ tablespoons butter in small pieces. Taste and adjust the seasoning.

To serve, place 1 veal medaillion on each of 4 heated serving plates, and top with a spoonful of sauce. The morels make their own side dish, or you may serve this with Carrot Mousse (see recipe).

Sautéed Cubed Veal

SERVES 4

The flavors of this dish improve with sitting, so make it ahead and heat it up at serving time.

2 ½ pounds veal, cut from the leg
4 tablespoons olive oil
1 medium Spanish onion, chopped
½ cup diced celery
½ cup diced green pepper
2 ½ tablespoons all-purpose flour
1 ½ cups dry white wine

1 cup Beef Stock (see recipe)
2 shallots, finely chopped
2 garlic cloves, finely chopped
1 sprig thyme, or ¼ teaspoon dried
1 bay leaf
2 tablespoons tomato paste
2 ripe tomatoes, peeled, seeded, and chopped
12 pitted green olives
Salt and freshly ground pepper to taste
1 tablespoon Cognac or brandy
⅓ cup chopped fresh parsley or chives

Cut the veal into 1-inch cubes. In a large skillet, heat the oil over medium heat. Add the veal cubes and brown evenly, stirring with a spoon and shaking the pan from time to time. Remove the meat and set aside.

Reduce the heat and add the onion, celery, and green pepper and cook until the onion is golden brown. Sprinkle the flour over the vegetables and cook 2 minutes more, stirring constantly. Then stir in the wine and stock, blending well. Add the shallots, garlic, thyme, bay leaf, tomato paste, and chopped tomatoes.

Bring to a boil and add the reserved veal. Reduce the heat and simmer, uncovered, about 40 minutes, or until the meat is tender. Add the olives, salt, and pepper and simmer an additional 10 minutes.

Skim any fat from surface, stir in the Cognac, and taste and adjust the seasoning. Sprinkle with parsley or chives and serve; or refrigerate, covered, to allow the flavors to develop, then reheat over low heat.

Veal in Tarragon-Mushroom Sauce

SERVES 4

This goes well with Dominique's Bouquets of Fresh Vegetables (see recipe).

Four 8-ounce veal scallops, cut into 1-inch slices and flattened to ¼-inch thickness
All-purpose flour seasoned with salt and pepper
½ pound mushrooms, cleaned and thickly sliced
6 tablespoons Clarified Butter (see recipe)
1 teaspoon fresh lemon juice
Salt and freshly ground pepper to taste
¼ cup finely chopped shallots
1 cup dry white wine
1 tablespoon chopped fresh tarragon, or ½ teaspoon dried
1 cup Beef Stock (see recipe)
2 tablespoons Cognac or brandy
1 tablespoon glace de viande, *or 1 bouillon cube (optional)*
Juice of 1 lemon
Watercress for garnish

Dust the veal with seasoned flour and set aside. Brown the mushrooms in 2 tablespoons clarified butter and 1 teaspoon lemon juice. Season lightly with salt and pepper, and set aside.

Cook the shallots in 2 tablespoons clarified butter until soft but not browned. Add the wine and tarragon and reduce to about 2 tablespoons. Stir in the beef stock and cook rapidly until slightly thickened, about 5 minutes. Add the reserved mushrooms and any liquid that has accumulated around them, and stir in the Cognac. Add *glace de viande* or bouillon cube, if desired. Stir in the juice of 1 lemon and salt and pepper to taste.

Bring to a simmer and keep warm while cooking the veal.

In a large skillet or sauté pan, heat the remaining 2 tablespoons clarified butter and cook the veal pieces until just tender, about 5 minutes. Season lightly with salt and pepper.

Spoon some of the sauce onto 4 individual serving plates, and arrange the veal slices on top. Spoon 1 tablespoon sauce on top of each portion of veal, and garnish with watercress.

Dominique's
Veal Stew

SERVES 4

1 ³⁄₄ pounds boneless white veal
¹⁄₃ cup sifted all-purpose flour
2 tablespoons vegetable oil
2 tablespoons butter
1 onion, finely chopped
12 small mushrooms with stems
2 cups dry white wine
2 ¹⁄₂ cups White Veal Stock or Chicken Stock (see recipes)
1 bay leaf
3 carrots, finely sliced
3 stalks celery, finely sliced
12 pitted green imported olives
1 cup heavy cream
2 tablespoons sour cream
³⁄₄ teaspoon strong Dijon mustard
1 teaspoon lemon juice
Salt and freshly ground pepper to taste

Cut the veal into 1 ¹⁄₂-inch cubes. Place flour in a paper bag; add the veal, and shake gently to dust the veal entirely with flour.

Heat the oil and 1 tablespoon butter in a deep cast-iron

skillet. Add the veal and cook over medium heat until brown. Remove the veal and set aside.

Remove fat from the skillet. Melt the remaining 1 tablespoon butter in the same pan, add the onion, and sauté until tender. Add the mushrooms, cook 1 minute, and then add wine and stir. Add the stock and the bay leaf and bring to a simmer. Add veal. Reduce heat and simmer gently, covered, about 1 hour. Remove bay leaf and discard.

Add the carrots, celery, and olives. Simmer another 10 to 12 minutes.

In a small bowl, blend the cream with the sour cream and mustard, and stir in 3 tablespoons of the cooking liquid. Return all to skillet, stir to combine, and add lemon juice, salt, and pepper. Taste and adjust seasoning. Simmer until heated through (do *not* boil).

Kidney Sauté with Madeira

SERVES 4

Served in France with mashed potatoes, we also serve it with green beans and Madeira Sauce.

1 ½ pounds veal or lamb kidneys (3 to 4 veal kidneys; 4 to 6 lamb kidneys)
1 tablespoon vegetable oil
3 tablespoons butter
2 tablespoons all-purpose flour
4 tablespoons Madeira
⅔ cup White Veal Stock (see recipe)
3 tablespoons heavy cream
Salt and freshly ground pepper to taste
2 tablespoons chopped fresh parsley
Madeira Sauce (see recipe)

Rinse the kidneys and pat dry. Skin them, cutting away all membranes and cutting out the cores with a kitchen shears. If using veal kidneys, cut into ½-inch slices; if using lamb kidneys, cut in half.

Heat the oil in a sauté pan over medium-high heat and add 1 tablespoon butter. When the butter foams, add the kidneys and cook, turning frequently, until browned all over, about 2 to 3 minutes. Sprinkle the kidneys with flour and shake the pan to coat them evenly. Remove the pan from the heat, pour in the Madeira, and flame. When the alcohol has evaporated, return the pan to the heat, pour in the stock, and bring to a boil, stirring. Simmer 4 to 5 minutes, until the kidneys are cooked but still pink in the center.

Remove the pan from the heat and stir in remaining 2 tablespoons butter in small pieces, shaking the pan to incorporate thoroughly. Add the cream, salt, and pepper and heat briefly, but *do not boil.*

Transfer the kidneys to a serving platter or individual plates, and pour the sauce over them; sprinkle with parsley and pass the Madeira Sauce alongside in a sauceboat.

Veal Kidneys in Mustard Sauce

SERVES 4

1 pound veal kidneys
Salt and freshly ground pepper to taste
4 tablespoons butter
2 tablespoons oil
¾ cup sliced fresh mushrooms
¼ cup finely chopped onion
4 shallots, finely chopped
2 tablespoons strong Dijon mustard
¼ cup dry sherry
½ cup Crème Fraîche (see recipe)
4 tablespoons chopped fresh parsley

Rinse the kidneys under cold water, pat dry, and cut away all membranes. Slice the kidneys ¾-inch thick, dust with salt and pepper, and set aside.

In a heavy skillet, heat the butter and oil to sizzling over medium-high heat. Add the kidneys and cook until golden brown, then remove from pan and reserve. Add the mushrooms, onion, and shallots to the pan and cook until tender. Remove with a slotted spoon and reserve.

Discard the fat in the pan and add the mustard and sherry. Cook over high heat for 2 minutes, remove the pan from the heat and add the kidneys and reserved vegetables. Return the pan to medium heat, bring to a simmer, and stir in the crème fraîche, blend well, and add the parsley. *Do not boil.* Taste and adjust seasoning, and serve immediately.

Baked Lamb Chops

SERVES 4

This recipe was given to me by one of the customers of our Washington, D.C., restaurant.

4 tablespoons butter, or more as needed
2 tablespoons vegetable oil
4 lamb chops (about 1 ½ inches thick)
2 medium onions, thinly sliced
2 garlic cloves, minced
1 cup Beef Stock (see recipe)
Salt and freshly ground pepper to taste
4 medium potatoes

Preheat the oven to 400°F.

Melt 2 tablespoons butter with the vegetable oil in a skillet and heat until foamy. Add the lamb chops and brown well on both sides, adding more butter if needed. Remove the chops and set aside. Add 2 tablespoons butter to the skillet, melt, and add the onions and garlic. Stir to loosen the particles from the bottom of the pan, and cook slowly for 2 minutes.

In a baking dish large enough to hold the chops, place the softened onion and garlic and spread into an even layer. Place the chops on top, add ½ cup stock, and season with salt and pepper. Place the baking dish, uncovered, in the oven and bake 30 minutes.

Peel the potatoes and slice thinly. Place over the chops, covering the meat completely. Pour the remaining ½ cup stock over, sprinkle with salt and pepper, and return to the oven for 30 minutes, or until the potatoes are soft, basting occasionally during baking.

Lamb Chops with Horseradish– Sour Cream Sauce

SERVES 4

Serve this rich dish with simple vegetables, such as steamed green beans, snow peas, or artichoke hearts.

8 small lamb chops (about 1 inch thick)
Salt and freshly ground pepper to taste
1 cup sour cream
4 tablespoons prepared horseradish
1 teaspoon chopped fresh dill or scallions
2 tablespoons minced fresh parsley
1 teaspoon paprika

Preheat the broiler.

Season the lamb chops with salt and pepper and broil to

desired doneness. While the chops are cooking, combine the remaining ingredients and stir well to blend. Serve the broiled lamb chops with the horseradish–sour cream sauce on the side.

Lamb Chops in Yogurt Marinade

SERVES 4

The lamb chops must be marinated overnight, so plan ahead. They go well with Rice Pilaf (see recipe).

8 lean thick lamb chops
1 cup plain yogurt
4 garlic cloves, crushed and minced
1 teaspoon minced fresh ginger
2 tablespoons fresh lemon juice
1 tablespoon paprika
1 pinch of salt
4 tablespoons olive oil

Trim the fat from the lamb chops. In a glass bowl, combine the yogurt, garlic, ginger, lemon juice, paprika, and salt. Add the lamb chops to marinade, coat well, cover, and refrigerate overnight.

When ready to cook the lamb chops, preheat the broiler. Remove the lamb chops from the marinade and brush both sides with olive oil. Broil about 5 minutes on each side for medium, less for rare meat.

Roasted Racks of Lamb Dominique

SERVES 4

This is Dominique's number-one specialty. We served 75,000 in Washington, D.C., in 1986, and 55,000 in Miami Beach! The racks marinate for 24 hours before cooking.

2 racks of lamb (6 chops each), trimmed

FOR THE MARINADE

1 teaspoon each salt and freshly ground pepper
2 tablespoons red wine vinegar
2 cups olive oil
Juice of 2 lemons
1 1/2 cups dry white wine
4 garlic cloves, crushed
1/2 teaspoon dried oregano
1 sprig thyme, or 1/4 teaspoon dried
2 bay leaves, crumbled
6 peppercorns

TO ROAST THE LAMB

1 teaspoon each salt and pepper
2 1/2 tablespoons olive oil

FOR THE BREAD CRUMB CRUST

6 tablespoons fine dry bread crumbs
6 tablespoons minced fresh parsley
2 garlic cloves, minced
2 teaspoons Dijon mustard
3 egg yolks, lightly beaten

TO FINISH COOKING

1 medium onion, chopped
³/₄ cup chopped celery
1 sprig thyme, or ¹/₄ teaspoon dried
1 bay leaf
2 large carrots, finely chopped
¹/₂ cup dry white wine

Place the racks of lamb in a large deep pan and dust with salt and pepper. Combine all remaining marinade ingredients, and pour over the lamb. Cover and refrigerate for at least 24 hours, turning occasionally.

Preheat the oven to 400°F.

In a large roasting pan, place 1 teaspoon each salt and pepper and the olive oil. Place the racks of lamb in the pan, fat side down, and roast 10 minutes.

While the lamb is cooking, combine the ingredients for the bread crumb crust and mix to a smooth paste.

Remove the lamb from the oven and let sit 5 minutes. With your hands, apply the bread crumb mixture to the outside of the racks of lamb, pressing firmly to make the mixture adhere to the meat. The crust should be about ¹/₃ inch thick. Return the lamb to the oven and cook 10 minutes more.

Add the onion, celery, thyme, bay leaf, and carrots to the pan and continue baking 20 to 25 minutes. For rare meat, a meat thermometer should read 140°F. Remove the racks of lamb to a serving platter and keep warm.

Drain all fat from the roasting pan and add the wine. Place the pan on top of the stove across 2 burners and bring the contents to a boil, scraping the bottom and sides of pan to dislodge all particles. Cook about 2 minutes and strain, discarding the solids. Skim off any fat, taste and adjust the seasoning, and serve with racks of lamb cut into chops.

Shish Kebab Dominique

SERVES 6

This is a very popular item on our lunch menu. Here again, the lamb must be marinated in advance. Serve it with Rice Pilaf (see recipe).

3 pounds lean lamb, preferably from the leg, cut into 2-inch cubes
3/4 cup olive oil
6 tablespoons lemon juice
1 1/2 onions, thinly sliced
1/2 cup chopped fresh parsley
3 garlic cloves, minced
Salt and freshly ground pepper to taste
4 sprigs thyme, or 1 teaspoon dried
1/2 teaspoon ground cumin
2 small firm ripe tomatoes, cut crosswise in 4 slices
1 large green pepper, seeded and quartered
6 large mushrooms, stems removed
4 tablespoons heavy cream or Clarified Butter (see recipe)

Place the lamb in a large bowl. Blend the olive oil and lemon juice with the sliced onions and all the herbs and spices, and pour over lamb, mixing well. Marinate in the refrigerator for 24 hours or more, turning the meat occasionally.

Preheat the broiler.

Remove the lamb from the marinade, and thread with the vegetables on skewers. Brush the lamb with cream or clarified butter, and broil 5 inches from the source of heat, turning the skewers to cook evenly. Broil about 10 to 12 minutes, or until the vegetables are done and the meat is rare. Slide the meat and vegetables off the skewers onto a bed of rice, and serve on individual plates.

Pork Chops with Mustard Sauce

SERVES 4

2 tablespoons butter
2 tablespoons vegetable oil
4 loin pork chops (1 inch thick)
Salt and freshly ground pepper to taste
1 egg yolk
1 tablespoon Dijon mustard
¼ cup heavy cream
½ cup dry white wine
1 garlic clove, mashed
1 teaspoon chopped fresh tarragon
1 teaspoon Cognac or brandy
3 teaspoons chopped fresh tarragon or chives for garnish

In a heavy skillet, melt the butter and heat to sizzling, then add the oil. Add the pork chops and brown well on both sides. Season the chops with salt and pepper. Cover, reduce the heat, and simmer 15 minutes.

While the chops are cooking, prepare the sauce flavorings. In a small bowl, beat together the egg yolk and mustard. Stir in the cream and set aside.

Remove the chops to a warm serving platter and keep warm. Turn up the heat under the skillet, pour in the wine, and scrape up all the browned bits from the bottom. Add the garlic, tarragon, and a little salt and pepper; boil 1 minute. Remove the skillet from the heat, add the mustard sauce, and stir for a few seconds. Return to the heat, stirring until the sauce thickens. Do not allow it to boil. Add the Cognac or brandy. Taste and adjust the seasoning.

To serve, spoon the sauce over the cooked pork chops, and sprinkle with tarragon or chives.

Baked Pork Chops

SERVES 4

This is a classic French dish.

8 pork chops, trimmed of fat
Salt and freshly ground pepper to taste
2 large onions
2 pounds potatoes
4 tablespoons butter
2 tablespoons vegetable oil
3 sprigs thyme, or 3/4 teaspoon dried
2 garlic cloves, crushed
1 3/4 cups Chicken Stock (see recipe)
1/2 cup dry white wine
1/3 cup grated Parmesan
2/3 cup chopped fresh parsley for garnish

Preheat the oven to 425°F.

Dust both sides of the pork chops with salt and pepper, and set aside. Slice the onions thinly and reserve. Peel the potatoes and slice thinly, then submerge in cold water until ready to use.

In a large skillet, heat the butter to sizzling, and add the oil. Place the chops in the pan and brown about 4 minutes on each side. Remove the chops and set aside. Add the onions to the skillet and cook over medium heat until tender and lightly browned.

In a buttered baking dish, layer half the onions. Place the browned pork chops on top of the onions. Drain the potatoes and mix with the thyme, garlic, chicken stock, wine, and the remaining onions; distribute over the chops. Dust with salt and pepper.

Place the baking dish on top of the stove and bring the contents to a boil. Cook 1 minute, then place in the oven and bake 35 minutes, or until potatoes are tender.

Remove the pan from oven and preheat the broiler. Discard the garlic and thyme sprigs, if used. Sprinkle the top with Parmesan, and place under the broiler to brown. Distribute the parsley over the top and serve.

Poultry and Stuffings

At Dominique's, we serve a tremendous variety of foods. But we make a special dinner for pre-theater guests, featuring roasted chicken accompanied by many of our other special dishes. And, of course, at Thanksgiving we serve beautiful turkeys with our Rice and Oyster Stuffing and all the trimmings. You'll find these recipes for chicken and stuffings on the pages that follow. But not all poultry dishes are uncomplicated and familiar affairs. Our Chicken Stew in White Wine with Chanterelle Sauce is simple to prepare, yet makes an elegant presentation. And Mrs. Ronald W. Reagan's Baja Chicken, which we serve at Dominique's with a few minor changes, takes just minutes to prepare.

No matter which dish you choose to prepare, remember that in all cases you must buy only the freshest ingredients. The texture, flavor, and, ultimately, the quality of any dish depend primarily on the raw ingredients. If your ingredients are the finest available, it is a simple matter to follow any recipe and achieve outstanding results. If you wish, you can add or subtract a little something to give the dish your own special touch. After all, the dish will be judged on its own merits, not on how closely you have duplicated any given recipe. Perfection should be your goal; do not be afraid to be inventive.

Baja, California, Chicken

SERVES 4

Dominique's serves my variation of the recipe Mrs. Ronald W. Reagan provided the board of the National Symphony Orchestra for their fund-raising cookbook.

4 chicken breasts, boned and skinned
Salt and freshly ground pepper to taste
4 garlic cloves, crushed
4 tablespoons olive oil
4 tablespoons tarragon vinegar
1/2 cup dry sherry
4 tablespoons chopped fresh tarragon

Preheat the oven to 375°F.

Dust the chicken with salt and pepper. Heat the garlic, oil, and vinegar in a large skillet. Bring to a simmer, add the chicken, and cook over medium heat, turning the chicken from time to time, until both sides are golden brown and tender.

Turn out all the ingredients from the skillet into a baking dish. Remove the garlic and discard. Pour the sherry over the chicken and place in the oven for 10 minutes. Sprinkle with chopped fresh tarragon, and serve with the rice or potatoes of your choice.

Chicken Dorothy

SERVES 4 TO 6 AS A MAIN COURSE; 8 AS A FIRST COURSE

This recipe is from a friend, a real Southern belle, who enjoys her life in North Carolina. Remember to plan ahead, since the chicken must be marinated at least 24 hours.

2 whole chickens, cut into 16 serving pieces
6 garlic cloves, finely chopped
3/4 cup olive oil
Juice of 1 lemon
1 cup chopped scallions
Salt and freshly ground pepper to taste
1 1/2 cups honey

Combine the chicken with the garlic, olive oil, lemon juice, scallions, salt, and pepper in a large bowl and refrigerate, covered, for 24 hours, turning the chicken from time to time.

Drain the chicken and discard the marinade.

Preheat the oven to 375°F.

Place the chicken pieces in a baking pan and bake about 45 minutes, until done. Remove the chicken pieces from the pan and let cool about 5 minutes at room temperature.

Preheat the broiler.

Place the chicken pieces in deep pan. Pour about 1 cup honey over, and turn the pieces so that all sides are coated. Place the chicken under the hot broiler and brown until the skin is golden and crisp, brushing the chicken with the remaining 1/2 cup honey while broiling. Keep the chicken in a heated oven until all the pieces are evenly browned. Serve hot as an appetizer or main course.

Chicken Fingers with Honey

SERVES 6 TO 8

We serve this at Dominique's as a lunch special, with fresh vegetables on the side.

4 pounds frying chicken, cut into 8 serving pieces
Salt and freshly ground pepper to taste
2 tablespoons olive oil
1 orange, quartered, with seeds removed and peel set aside
Juice of 1 orange
1 1/2 tablespoons grated fresh ginger
1 cup dry red wine
1 teaspoon red wine vinegar
1/2 cup honey
1 tablespoon cornstarch, dissolved in 2 tablespoons water
4 tablespoons chopped fresh parsley

Preheat the oven to 350°F.

Season the chicken with salt and pepper. Heat the oil in a Dutch oven or stovetop casserole dish. Sauté the chicken until golden brown all over, about 6 minutes on each side. Drain off the fat. Add the orange pieces, orange juice, and ginger. Bake, covered, about 45 minutes, or until the chicken is done.

Remove the chicken pieces from the Dutch oven or casserole and set aside. Add the wine, vinegar, honey, and orange peel to the pan juices. Bring to a boil. Reduce the heat and simmer until the sauce is reduced to about 1 1/3 cups. Remove the orange peel. Add the cornstarch mixture. Stir, bring to a boil, and simmer about 1 minute. Taste and adjust the seasoning. Pour sauce over chicken, sprinkle with parsley, and serve immediately.

Chicken Breasts with Boursin Cheese

SERVES 6

6 whole chicken breasts, boned and skinned
Salt and freshly ground pepper to taste
2 packages (about 12 ounces) Boursin cheese
3 eggs, lightly beaten
1 1/2 cups bread crumbs
1/3 cup butter, melted
1/3 cup dry white wine
Fresh watercress for garnish

Preheat the oven to 375°F.

Split the chicken breasts and flatten each piece between 2 layers of wax paper. Season with salt and pepper and set aside.

Divide the cheese into 12 parts. Roll the cheese into cylindrical shapes, then place 1 cheese cylinder in middle of each chicken breast, and roll the breast around the cheese to cover completely. Dip the rolled-up chicken breasts in egg, then roll in bread crumbs. Place in a baking dish, seam side down. Cover with melted butter and add the wine. Bake 30 minutes, or until done, basting occasionally. Garnish with watercress.

Chicken Piquante

SERVES 4

This recipe was selected by the Inaugural Committee as the entrée to serve to President and Mrs. Ronald W. Reagan at the Inaugural luncheon at the Capitol Rotunda. The recipe originated with Mrs. William French Smith. We have served this unusual recipe at Dominique's in Washington, D.C., often, and it is always well received by our guests.

4 chicken breasts, boned and skinned
4 tablespoons butter
¼ cup sifted all-purpose flour
6 tablespoons capers, drained
½ cup dry white wine
Salt and freshly ground pepper to taste
4 tablespoons chopped fresh parsley for garnish

Cut the chicken into strips. Melt the butter in a large frying pan. Coat the chicken pieces entirely with flour, and sauté in the butter until tender and golden brown on all sides. Add the capers and white wine and bring to a simmer. Remove the chicken and keep warm. Reduce the liquid to about half. Pour over the chicken and season with salt and pepper. Serve garnished with chopped parsley.

Chicken Stew in White Wine with Chanterelle Sauce

SERVES 4

1 chicken (about 6 to 7 pounds), cut up into serving pieces
Salt and freshly ground pepper to taste
½ cup sifted all-purpose flour
¼ cup butter
1 tablespoon vegetable oil
3 carrots, coarsely chopped
3 celery stalks with leaves, coarsely chopped
1 large onion, coarsely chopped
2 garlic cloves, mashed
4 cups Chicken Stock (see recipe)
2⅓ cups dry white wine
3 bouquets garnis (see p. 32)
Chanterelle Sauce (see following recipe)

Season the chicken pieces with salt and pepper and toss with flour. Melt the butter in a large casserole over medium-high heat. When the butter sizzles, add the oil. Sauté the chicken pieces until golden brown, about 3 minutes per side. Add the vegetables and garlic and stir all the ingredients, including the chicken, with a wooden spoon for about 3 to 4 minutes, to blend. Add the chicken stock and wine, bring the liquid to a boil, and add the bouquets garnis. Reduce the heat, cover, and simmer gently for about 1 ½ hours, or until the chicken is tender.

Remove the chicken and set aside. Strain the juice, discarding all solids. Skim the fat from the stock, and use the stock to prepare the Chanterelle Sauce. Place the chicken on a serving platter or in a bowl, pour the sauce over, and serve immediately.

Chanterelle Sauce

MAKES ABOUT 2 1/2 CUPS

¼ cup butter
¼ cup sifted all-purpose flour
Reserved chicken stock (from preparing the chicken)
2 cups heavy cream, blended with 2 egg yolks
4 tablespoons finely chopped fresh parsley, or 2 tablespoons chopped fresh tarragon
⅓ pound chanterelles, whole or cut into bite-size pieces, rinsed and patted dry

Melt the butter in a saucepan over medium heat. Add the flour, stirring constantly, and cook over medium-high heat about 3 minutes. Gradually pour in the reserved chicken stock, blending well with a whisk. Bring to a simmer, then remove from the heat. Gradually add the cream-yolks mixture to the stock mixture, stirring constantly. Use a whisk to blend all the ingredients well. Add the parsley or tarragon and chanterelles. Return to the heat and bring to a simmer, but *do not boil.* Serve at once with Chicken Stew in White Wine (preceding recipe).

Roasted Chicken Dominique

SERVES 4

We serve a lot of roasted chickens at Dominique's. You'll find this recipe simple to prepare and very, very tasty.

One 3- to 4-pound roasting chicken
3 tablespoons butter, at room temperature
Juice of 1 lemon
Salt and freshly ground pepper to taste
1 small Spanish onion, peeled
4 tablespoons melted butter
1 tablespoon peanut oil
1 large onion, thickly sliced
1 large carrot, cut up
1 celery stalk, cut up
1 turnip, peeled and quartered
4 sprigs parsley, chopped
12 large mushrooms
1 cup Chicken Stock (see recipe)

Preheat the oven to 425°F.

Rinse the chicken and pat dry. Blend the softened butter, lemon juice, salt, and pepper. Brush the inside of the chicken with this mixture. Place the Spanish onion inside the cavity, and truss the chicken with white kitchen string. Combine the melted butter and peanut oil, and brush the outside of the chicken with half this mixture.

Place the chicken in a roasting pan, breast side down, and roast 15 minutes. Brush the bird with butter and oil, and roast 15 minutes more.

Reduce the heat to 375°F. Place all the vegetables, except the mushrooms, in the roasting pan. Turn the chicken breast side up and baste with the remaining butter-oil mixture. Roast

35 minutes, basting with pan juices from time to time. Ten minutes before the chicken is done, add the parsley and mushrooms to pan.

When the chicken is done, remove the bird and mushrooms from the roasting pan. Reserve the mushrooms; discard the other vegetables. Cut the string, remove and discard the Spanish onion, and let the bird cool while you make the sauce.

To make the sauce, add the chicken stock to the roasting pan, scrape the bottom and sides of pan to loosen any particles, and bring pan juices to a boil on top of the stove. Boil 3 minutes. Strain the juices through a sieve, and skim off the fat. Taste and adjust the seasoning.

Carve the chicken, and serve with the sauce and reserved mushrooms.

Southern-Style Chicken

SERVES 4

1 large frying chicken
1/2 pound very lean salt pork, cut into 2-inch strips
6 thick lemon slices
1/2 cup dry white wine
1 large carrot, chopped
1 large onion, sliced
2 sprigs thyme, or 1/2 teaspoon dried
1 bay leaf
1 tablespoon chopped fresh parsley
1 teaspoon salt
1 teaspoon freshly ground pepper
1/2 cup Chicken Stock (see recipe)

Rinse the chicken and pat dry. Truss as if you were going to roast the bird.

Lay salt pork strips across the bottom of a roasting pan and lay lemon slices over them. Add the wine and place over low heat. As soon as the pork starts to melt, add the carrot, onion, and all the herbs and seasonings. Place the chicken in the roasting pan and add the chicken stock.

Cover the pan loosely and bring to a boil. Reduce the heat and simmer about 1 hour, or until the chicken is tender, basting with the liquid in pan every 15 minutes.

Remove the chicken from the pan and allow to cool for 5 to 10 minutes. Skim the fat from the sauce, and discard the solids. Serve the chicken with sauce from the pan, accompanied by Creamy Coleslaw and Hush Puppies (see recipes).

Roasted Chicken with Sausage Stuffing

SERVES 4

Serve this with Chicken Liver Ramekins with Light Tomato Sauce (see following recipe).

FOR THE STUFFING

Liver from chicken being roasted
1 pound of your favorite sausage (pork, beef, or both)
1 onion, finely chopped
2 garlic cloves, finely minced
2 cups cubed white bread
1/3 cup freshly grated Parmesan
1/3 cup chopped fresh parsley
Salt and freshly ground pepper to taste
4 to 5 tablespoons Chicken Stock (see recipe)

1 roasting chicken (4 to 5 pounds)
4 slices of bacon
1 cup Chicken Stock (see recipe)

Preheat the oven to 350°F.

To prepare the stuffing, remove the liver from the chicken and set aside. Remove the skin from the sausage. Place the sausage meat in a heavy skillet and cook over moderate-high heat for 3 minutes. Add the onion, liver, and garlic. Cook 1 or 2 minutes. Remove from the heat. Discard the fat. Add the bread, Parmesan, parsley, salt, and pepper and enough chicken stock to moisten the dressing.

Fill the cavity of the chicken with the stuffing. Put the chicken in a roasting pan and place the bacon slices over the breast. Roast the chicken approximately 1 ½ hours, or until done (meat thermometer should register 175°F).

Place the chicken on a serving platter and keep warm. Skim the fat from the roasting pan and discard bacon slices. Add the stock to the pan and cook on top of the stove over high heat, stirring well to blend all the drippings. Bring to a boil and reduce the liquid by half. Carve the chicken, and serve with the stuffing and gravy.

Chicken Liver Ramekins with Light Tomato Sauce

SERVES 4

One of our favorite side dishes with our roasted chicken or any simple chicken dish.

3/4 cup heavy cream
6 ounces fresh chicken livers
2 eggs
1 egg yolk
¼ garlic clove, very finely chopped
Freshly grated nutmeg to taste
Salt and freshly ground pepper to taste

FOR THE LIGHT TOMATO SAUCE

2 tablespoons butter
4 shallots, chopped
2 garlic cloves, crushed
2 pounds tomatoes, peeled and seeded
Salt and freshly ground pepper to taste

Preheat the oven to 375°F.

Fill a roasting pan with about an inch of boiling water and set on top of the stove. Generously butter four ½-cup ramekins. In a pan, bring the cream to a boil. Rinse the chicken livers under cold water and drain on paper towels. Purée the chicken livers in a blender or food processor with the eggs and extra egg yolk. Transfer the liver mixture to a bowl and add the cream gradually, whisking well after each addition. Add the chopped garlic, and season with nutmeg, salt, and pepper. Pour the liver purée into the ramekins, filling them not more than three-quarters full.

Put the ramekins in the water bath, bring to a simmer on top of the stove, and transfer to the preheated oven. Bake until a skewer inserted in the center of a ramekin comes out clean, about 30 to 35 minutes.

Meanwhile, prepare the tomato sauce. Melt the butter in a saucepan, add the shallots, and cook until soft but not brown. Add the garlic, tomatoes, and salt and simmer, uncovered, until the tomatoes are very soft, about 30 minutes. Purée the sauce in a blender or food processor, then strain it back into the pan. Reduce over low heat, if necessary, until thick enough to coat the back of a wooden spoon. Season with salt and pepper.

Remove the ramekins from the oven and let rest 1 minute. Turn the ramekins out onto a platter or individual plates, and coat with the sauce.

Chicken Liver Casserole

SERVES 4

Serve this with a nice green salad for a hearty and healthy lunch or dinner.

¼ cup butter
2 tablespoons chopped onion
¾ cup chopped celery, with leaves
6 chicken livers (about 12 ounces total), cut in quarters
1½ cups sliced mushrooms
½ teaspoon salt
½ teaspoon freshly ground pepper
⅓ cup Chicken Stock (see recipe)
4 tablespoons dry white wine
3 cups cooked rice (cooked in chicken or beef broth)
3 tablespoons chopped fresh parsley or chives
½ cup grated Parmesan

In a heavy skillet, melt the butter to sizzling, then add the onion and celery. Cook 2 minutes, then reduce heat and add the livers, stirring constantly. Cook 2 minutes, then add the mushrooms, salt, pepper, chicken stock, and wine and simmer gently for 3 minutes more. Blend in the rice and heat gradually, stirring gently from time to time with a fork. Sprinkle with parsley or chives and Parmesan before serving.

Roasted Stuffed Canada Goose

SERVES 4

1 Canada goose (8 to 10 pounds), cleaned
1 medium head red cabbage
2 large tart apples, peeled, cored, and chopped
1/2 cup chopped fresh mushrooms
1/2 cup chopped ham
1 egg
1 tablespoon caraway seeds
1 bay leaf, crushed
2 sprigs thyme, or 1/2 teaspoon dried
Salt and freshly ground pepper to taste
2 cups dry red wine
4 celery stalks, chopped
4 onions, coarsely chopped
Green Peppercorn Sauce for Fowl (see recipe)

Preheat the oven to 425°F.

Place enough water to cover goose in a large stockpot. Bring to a boil, add the goose, and simmer 10 minutes; then remove goose from the water and let cool. Rinse in cold water and pat dry.

Shred the cabbage, and boil 5 minutes in salted water. Drain and let the cabbage cool. Mix the cabbage with the apples, mushrooms, ham, and egg. Add the caraway seeds, bay leaf, thyme, salt, and pepper. Stuff the goose with this mixture.

Place the goose in a roasting pan and pour the red wine over. Add the celery and onions to the pan. Roast 15 minutes; then lower heat to 350°F. Cover the pan tightly with heavy-duty aluminum foil and continue roasting 3 1/2 hours, or until tender. Serve with Green Peppercorn Sauce for Fowl.

Deviled Roast
Rock Cornish Game Hens

SERVES 4

This recipe is popular on our annual television appearances in Florida. It's good served with sweet potatoes.

4 tablespoons soy sauce
3 tablespoons honey
1 tablespoon cider vinegar
Two 1 1/2-pound Rock Cornish game hens, halved, backbones removed, and patted dry
1 to 2 tablespoons olive oil
Salt and freshly ground pepper to taste
2 tablespoons Dijon mustard
Watercress sprigs for garnish

In a large shallow bowl, whisk together the soy sauce, honey, and vinegar. Add the hen halves and turn them to coat with the marinade. Let the hens marinate, skin side down, at room temperature for at least 3 hours, or covered in the refrigerator overnight.

Preheat the oven to 425°F.

Transfer the hens, skin side up, to the foil-lined rack of a broiling pan, reserving the marinade. Brush the hens with the oil, and season with salt and pepper. Roast for 15 minutes.

While the hens are roasting, bring the reserved marinade to a boil in a small saucepan and cook it, stirring occasionally, until reduced by half. Remove the pan from the heat and whisk in the mustard.

Brush the hens liberally with the mustard-marinade mixture and continue to roast them, basting one more time with the mustard mixture, for 10 to 15 minutes, or until the juices run clear when a thigh is pricked with a skewer (170°F. on an instant-read meat thermometer).

Transfer the hens to a heated platter with a slotted spatula, arrange sweet potatoes on the platter, if desired, and garnish with the watercress.

Stuffing for Poultry

MAKES 2 CUPS

1 whole chicken liver
1/4 cup butter, melted
1/4 onion, diced
1 celery stalk with leaves, diced
1 garlic clove, minced
1/2 cup grated carrot
2 cups cubed day-old bread
1/2 apple, peeled, cored, and chopped
1 tablespoon chopped fresh sage leaves
1 1/2 teaspoons chopped fresh parsley
1/2 teaspoon salt
1/4 teaspoon pepper
1/2 teaspoon dried thyme
3 tablespoons raisins
1 1/2 tablespoons dry sherry

In a skillet or saucepan, sauté the liver in 1 tablespoon melted butter until the inside just loses its pinkness, then chop and place in a large mixing bowl. In the same pan, sauté the onion, celery, garlic, and grated carrot until the onion is translucent. Add the sautéed vegetables to the chopped liver in the mixing bowl. Add the bread, apple, sage, parsley, salt, pepper, thyme, and raisins. Add the rest of the melted butter and the sherry and stir to combine well.

Oyster Stuffing for Turkey

MAKES ENOUGH TO STUFF AN 8- TO 15-POUND TURKEY

1/2 cup butter
2 cups finely chopped onions
1 green pepper, seeded and finely chopped
1 red pepper, seeded and finely chopped
2 cups chopped celery leaves
1 teaspoon dried sage
1 teaspoon poultry seasoning
16 cups cubed stale bread
1 quart oysters with their liquor
Salt and freshly ground pepper to taste
Chicken Stock (see recipe), as needed

Melt the butter in a large skillet. Add the vegetables and cook about 5 minutes. Remove from the heat and add the remaining ingredients, using enough chicken stock to give the stuffing a good consistency. Taste and adjust the seasoning.

Rice and Oyster Stuffing
Dominique

MAKES ENOUGH TO STUFF AN 8- TO 15-POUND TURKEY, 2 LARGE CHICKENS, OR 4 WHOLE FISH

We use this to stuff our Thanksgiving turkeys in both Miami Beach and Washington, D.C.

143

¹/₂ cup butter
10 scallions, chopped
2 cups chopped celery
1 cup diced green peppers
1 cup diced red peppers
1 cup diced onion
1 quart oysters with their liquor
3 cups cooked rice
2 to 2¹/₂ cups Chicken Stock (see recipe)
1 cup chopped fresh parsley
Salt and freshly ground pepper to taste

Melt the butter in a large frying pan. Add all vegetables and cook over medium heat about 5 minutes, or until tender. Add the oysters and their liquor, then stir in the rice, blend, and add 2 cups chicken stock. Add additional chicken stock if needed to moisten sufficiently. Add the parsley and salt and pepper. Taste and adjust the seasoning.

Sausage Stuffing for Fowl

MAKES ABOUT 3 CUPS

Try this stuffing with goose, pheasant, or duck. This recipe provides enough stuffing for a large goose; for smaller birds such as duck or pheasant, reduce the quantities according to the size and number of birds you intend to prepare for roasting.

2 medium onions, chopped
1/2 cup unsalted butter, at room temperature
2 tablespoons oil
1 cup good beef or pork sausage meat
1 cup stale or toasted bread crumbs
1/2 cup finely chopped celery hearts
1 small apple, cored, peeled, and chopped
2 teaspoons dried thyme
2 tablespoons chopped fresh parsley
2 tablespoons chopped scallions (white part only)
Salt and freshly ground pepper to taste

Sauté the onions in the butter until tender and golden brown; remove from the heat and transfer to a large bowl. Heat the oil in a heavy skillet and cook the sausage meat quickly, just enough to cook the meat. Drain off the fat. Add the sausage meat to the bowl and combine with the onions; add all the remaining ingredients and stir well. Taste and adjust the seasoning. Let cool before stuffing the bird of your choice.

Fish
and Seafood

Buying fish calls for special attention. First, always buy *fresh* fish. If your recipe calls for a specific fish that cannot be found fresh, substitute another fresh fish or choose a different recipe. And always buy fish from a reputable dealer, one who allows you to examine the fish closely. The signs of freshness are unmistakable:

- A pleasant, clean smell of the lake, river, or ocean
- Bright, clear eyes
- Red, shiny gills
- Tight scales
- Firm, elastic flesh that springs back when pressed with a finger.

If possible, avoid buying precut fish fillets, but if you do not have a choice, the fillets should be odorless and dry.

As for shellfish, lobsters and crabs must be able to bite you

146

hard when you buy them—that is, purchase them *live*. Clams, oysters, and mussels should be tightly closed and should feel heavy in your hand. This indicates the presence of liquid in the shells. Shrimp should be firm and almost odorless.

If you are cooking fish that you have just pulled from the water yourself, remember to remove the fish's digestive system as soon as it is caught. Rinse the fish in clear water and immediately place it on ice. For maximum freshness, keep the fish in your refrigerator no longer than one day before using.

The most important things to remember when handling and cooking fish are:

- Handle fish very gently, since bruised or punctured flesh and skin will deteriorate rapidly.

- Store fresh fish in the coolest part of your refrigerator, wrapped in heavy wax paper or other moistureproof paper and *under ice,* until ready to cook.

- Never rinse fish under *running* water. Dip the fish in icy salted water instead, and pat dry immediately with paper towels.

- If because of availability, you need to make a substitution in any recipe, always use a fat fish for another fat fish, a lean fish for another lean one.

- When cooking a whole fish, leave the head on if possible. It can always be removed later, if you prefer, before the fish is served. Leaving the head on seals in juices and keeps the fish moist.

- Use only the finest quality oil, wine, butter, herbs, et cetera, when cooking fish. Inferior-quality products will let you know immediately that you're doing something wrong. A fine fish deserves fine ingredients in any recipe.

- A small, pastry-type brush is ideal for distributing oil or butter evenly over fish.

- A long two-tined fork will work as your "magic wand" when you're checking to see if the fish flakes easily. It will cause little breakage in the fish, too.

147

- Slightly moistened salt applied to the hands and rinsed off with warm water will remove any fish odor from your skin. Slightly moistened salt rubbed on pots, knives, and other kitchen utensils—followed by a thorough rinsing with hot water—will remove any fish smell that remains. Oven pans, dishes, skillets, trays, et cetera, should be soaked in hot salted water as soon as they cool.

As you sample the recipes in this section, keep in mind that there are seven basic ways to cook fish:

1. *Poaching*—to cook in a simmering liquid
2. *Steaming*—to cook by steam generated by boiling water
3. *Baking*—to cook by dry heat
4. *Broiling*—to cook by dry heat that is direct, intense, and comes from only one source
5. *Charcoal broiling*—to cook over hot coals
6. *Deep-frying*—to cook in a deep layer of hot fat
7. *Pan-frying*—to cook in a small amount of fat over moderate heat.

Each of these cooking methods is represented in this collection.

No matter what method of preparation you select, handle the fish gently and do not overcook. Fish is cooked when the flesh becomes opaque. Another easy way to determine doneness is to pierce the thickest part of the flesh with a fork; if the fish flakes easily, it is fully cooked. Overcooking dries out the fish, makes it tough, and ruins its delicate flavor.

At Dominique's, we have most of our salmon brought in from Norway, where it is handled with extreme care. The salmon is no more than 24 hours old when it arrives. But I've had some personal experiences salmon fishing in Alaska that I'd like to relate to you. Read on—there's even a recipe included!

For four weeks during the annual migration of the Pacific salmon, also known as the king salmon or chinook, the area surrounding Alaska's Bristol Bay becomes one of the world's great fishing spots. Fishing in this region can be unbelievably intense. There, near the spawning grounds of the world's largest salmon run, surrounded by truly spectacular mountain scenery, you have all the ingredients for the ultimate fishing experience. I know, because for the past two years I've traveled to Alaska to try it for myself. Let me tell you, my friend, entering the Naknek River in a blowing cold rain is probably the wildest thrill I've ever had as a sport fisherman. There before me were what seemed like dozens of shiny beauties jumping clear of the water all around our boat. One look, and I knew I was in for the fishing adventure of a lifetime!

The village of King Salmon, situated 300 miles southwest of Anchorage and about 30 miles from Bristol Bay, is near Katmai National Monument. It is accessible only by plane. If it were not for the abundance of salmon in the local Naknek River, this tiny dot of a place would have been written off the map long ago. But if there's a better river for salmon than the Naknek, I'd like to know where it is.

At the height of the salmon run, from the last week in June to the third week in July, boat traffic on the river is so heavy that you'd swear you were in the middle of Times Square! Night and day the boats pass, each loaded with gear and carrying up to three eager anglers and a guide. The open flat-bottomed boats range from 14 to 16 feet and are fitted with outboard motors. They drift along the wide, rocky, fast-moving river and its adjoining streams, sometimes anchoring over the deep gravel beds where the female salmon bury their eggs.

The salmon here are plentiful, but also elusive and hard hitting. They show plenty of fight, and pose a tough challenge for any angler—not only because of their size and strength, but also because they do not travel in schools. Furthermore, their reproductive glands have swollen in anticipation of mating, blocking their digestive tract and therefore their appetite. They're simply not interested in your bait. In fact, most of the salmon that are landed are hooked at the side of the jaw as they thrash their heads in anger when bait is presented. Like the tarpon, the king jumps furiously in an attempt to throw off the hook or may swim around rocks to tangle and break the line. Regardless of your fishing skill, you can only count on bringing back one fish for every five that you hook.

If you want to be successful and obtain your daily limit of three king salmon, I recommend that you travel the river with experienced fishermen or guides who know the water, the tides, the winds, and the type of plugs to tie at the end of your line. I was fortunate to fish with retired Air Force General Jim Isbell, John Meek, and his friend General Preston. These three anglers have fished up and down the Naknek for the past ten years. If you want to learn how to locate and hook king salmon, you'll never find better teachers. They know every trick, and then some. In their company, I caught my limit every day and even landed one salmon that weighed 58 pounds! (The largest salmon on record originated from nearby Petersburg, Alaska, and weighed 120 pounds.) Average weight is between 15 and 40 pounds.

And now, let me digress a moment to give you a recipe Jim Isbell taught me. If you go salmon fishing, and have access to a smokehouse, you'll treasure this recipe as much as I do!

Smoked Salmon Isbell

SERVES 6 TO 8

2 pounds fillet of Alaskan salmon belly meat, boned and skinned
1/2 cup non-iodized salt

Rub the salmon with salt and refrigerate 4 hours. Rinse the fish in a pot of cold water to remove the excess salt. Refrigerate on racks 24 hours (this allows the salt to continue to penetrate without making the salmon too salty). Place the fish in a smoke-house and smoke at 90°F. for 5 to 6 hours. Allow the fish to return to room temperature, then wrap in aluminum foil and refrigerate until ready to serve. Slice the salmon very thin, and serve with dark rye bread.

When it comes to eating enjoyment, you can hardly surpass the delicate taste and eye appeal of fresh king salmon. So I've bunched all the salmon recipes together at the beginning of this chapter. In your local market, fresh king may be available on a seasonal basis only. You can certainly substitute another smaller Pacific variety, such as sockeye, coho, or pink. Canadian or Atlantic salmon may be more plentiful in some parts of the country and can be used in these recipes, too. Whatever you do, avoid buying frozen fish. Purchase your salmon from a reliable market and examine it for the unmistakable signs of freshness mentioned above.

The sturdy reddish meat of the salmon lends itself to a variety of preparations, from simple poaching or broiling to smoking or salt-curing. Velvety sauces and fresh vegetables figure in many recipes. I've included a sampling of my personal favorites. But first, you'll find a recipe for court bouillon, the all-purpose cooking liquid for absolutely any fish.

Plain Court Bouillon for Fish

MAKES 1 QUART

A basic poaching liquid, good with any fish.

For best results, poach the fish over low heat, allowing 10 minutes per pound of whole fish, or 8 minutes for fish fillets.

1 quart water
½ teaspoon salt
2 tablespoons red wine vinegar
2 lemon slices
1 onion, thinly sliced
6 sprigs parsley
1 bay leaf
4 peppercorns
1 whole clove
3 tablespoons sherry

Combine all the ingredients, except the sherry, in a stainless-steel pot and boil 15 minutes. Strain the liquid, discarding the lemon slices and vegetables. Stir in the sherry and let cool.

Court bouillon can also be frozen until needed. Strain before freezing. After each use it can be refrozen. When ready to use again, add enough water to make 1 quart liquid.

Baked Salmon
with Hollandaise Sauce

SERVES 4 TO 6

Baking is the most common method of salmon preparation and certainly one of the easiest. A whole fish can be baked either with or without stuffing. I like the taste of a combination of olive oil and garlic brushed liberally over the entire fish. Wrapping the fish in aluminum foil seals in the baking juices.

1 whole salmon (about 4 to 5 pounds), cleaned, gutted, tail and head removed
3 large onions, thinly sliced
2 lemons, thinly sliced
½ cup olive oil
3 large garlic cloves, finely chopped
5 sprigs parsley
2 tablespoons chopped fresh tarragon
Hollandaise Sauce (see following recipe)

Preheat the oven to 400°F.

Wash the salmon thoroughly and pat dry. Line a baking sheet with aluminum foil. Place the onions and lemon slices on the foil, and place the fish on top. Combine the olive oil and garlic, and brush over the fish. Spread parsley and tarragon over the fish. Fold the edges of the foil over the top and ends of the fish and seal. Bake 10 minutes per pound, or until the flesh flakes when touched with a fork. Serve with Hollandaise Sauce.

Hollandaise Sauce

MAKES 1 CUP

Hollandaise is served warm, not hot. It can be kept warm atop a double boiler for an hour.

3 tablespoons water
3 egg yolks
Salt and white pepper
6 ounces Clarified Butter (see recipe), warmed but not hot
Juice of ½ lemon

In a small heavy, round-bottomed saucepan, whisk the water and egg yolks with a little salt and pepper until light, about 30 seconds. Set the pan over very low heat and whisk constantly, until the mixture is creamy and thick enough to form a ribbon trail.

Remove from the heat and whisk in the tepid butter, a few drops at a time. When the sauce has started to thicken or emulsify, the butter can be added a little faster. When all the butter has been added, stir in the lemon juice. Taste and adjust the seasoning.

Sauce Mousseline: Whip ¼ cup heavy cream until stiff, then fold into the Hollandaise Sauce. Serve at once.

Mustard Sauce: Whisk 2 teaspoons Dijon mustard into the Hollandaise Sauce, and voilà! This is wonderful with fish, eggs, shellfish, and even kidneys.

Salmon Stuffed with Caviar

SERVES 6

Salmon is the big thing at Dominique's, and this recipe, just introduced, is taking business away from the racks of lamb!

Six 7-ounce salmon fillets
Juice of 3 lemons
6 ounces caviar (best quality you can afford)
Salt and freshly ground pepper to taste
½ cup sifted all-purpose flour
10 tablespoons Clarified Butter (see recipe)

FOR THE SAUCE

½ cup unsalted butter
1 celery stalk with leaves, finely chopped
4 shallots, finely chopped
10 ounces extra-dry white vermouth
1 quart heavy cream
Salt and freshly ground pepper to taste
6 mushrooms, cleaned, trimmed, and cut into thick slices

Preheat the oven to 350°F.

Using a sharp knife, make a small pocket in the thick part of each salmon fillet. Squeeze the juice of ½ lemon inside each pocket. Stuff each with 1 ounce caviar, and press gently to close up the hole. Sprinkle the fish with salt and pepper and dust with flour. Sauté in a skillet in the clarified butter over high heat for 2 minutes per side. Transfer the salmon to the oven and bake about 7 minutes, or until done. Set the fish aside on a warm platter and keep warm.

Discard the clarified butter from the frying pan. Add the unsalted butter to the pan and sauté the celery and shallots for about 5 minutes over medium heat, or until the vegetables are tender. Add the vermouth and, over low heat, simmer about 5 minutes, or until reduced by half. Add the heavy cream, and season with salt and pepper. Continue reducing the sauce over low heat until the sauce thickens and coats the back of a wooden spoon. Strain the sauce. Add the mushrooms, and taste and adjust the seasoning. Pour the sauce over the salmon fillets, and serve with boiled potatoes and snow peas.

NOTE: If you wish, you can get started making the sauce while the salmon is baking; or you can make the sauce first and keep it warm for a few minutes in the top of a double boiler, while you prepare and cook the salmon.

Salmon Baked in Paper

SERVES 2

This is a very big item on our menu in Washington, D.C.

2 fresh boneless salmon fillets (about 6 to 7 ounces each)
Salt and freshly ground pepper to taste
2 tablespoons finely chopped fresh dill
4 tablespoons butter, at room temperature, blended with 2 teaspoons finely
*   chopped celery leaves*
1/2 red pepper, cut into thin strips
1 carrot, cut into thin strips
18 to 20 precooked fresh string beans
1 large ripe tomato, peeled, seeded, and finely chopped
1 tablespoon olive oil
1/3 cup dry vermouth or dry white wine
1 teaspoon tarragon vinegar
1 branch fresh tarragon
1 egg yolk, lightly beaten

Preheat the oven to 450°F.

Dust each fillet with salt and pepper, and place on parchment paper. Sprinkle fresh dill on top of the fish. Spread the prepared butter on top. Arrange the red pepper and carrot strips and string beans evenly over the butter.

In a saucepan, combine the tomato, olive oil, and vermouth or white wine and bring to a quick boil. Add the tarragon vinegar and fresh tarragon. Continue cooking over high heat until the tomato mixture is reduced to the consistency of a thick tomato sauce. Add salt and pepper to taste. Remove from the heat and stir to cool to room temperature. Remove the tarragon and discard.

Spoon the sauce over the fish. Brush the parchment paper around fish with beaten egg yolk. Bring the 2 edges of paper together and seal tightly by folding both pieces, crimping the ends to seal completely. Lay each package in a shallow buttered baking dish and bake about 6 minutes. Serve at once, cutting the paper at the table.

Barbecued Salmon

SERVES 6

6 tablespoons soy sauce
1 cup fresh apple cider
½ cup dry white wine
3 tablespoons unsalted butter
2 large garlic cloves, crushed
1 salmon fillet (about 4 pounds), or six 7-ounce salmon steaks
Lemon slices for garnish
Fresh parsley or coriander for garnish

Combine the soy sauce, cider, and wine in a small stainless-steel saucepan. Bring quickly to a boil, reduce heat, and simmer 15 minutes. Add the butter and garlic, and continue simmering 30 minutes, or until you have about ⅔ cup liquid. Remove from the heat and let cool.

Rinse the salmon in cold water and pat dry. Brush half the marinade evenly over the salmon. Let stand at room temperature for 45 minutes. Brush a second time with the remaining marinade and let stand another 45 minutes.

Place the salmon on a hot grill. Cover with aluminum foil and bake until the fish is done, approximately 10 to 15 minutes, depending on thickness.

Serve garnished with lemon slices and parsley. A good sauce accompaniment for this dish is sour cream blended with fresh blueberries or raspberries.

NOTE: If using salmon steaks instead of fillets, brush each side of the steaks with marinade once, and let sit 45 minutes. Then proceed with cooking.

Potlatch Salmon

SERVES 4

This rich dish is like a pepper steak, using juniper berries in lieu of peppercorns. If you want to serve a vegetable, I recommend Dominique's Bouquets of Fresh Vegetables (see recipe).

1 tablespoon juniper berries (about 50 berries)
2 pounds king salmon, cut into four 8-ounce steaks
¼ cup olive oil
1½ teaspoons salt
Freshly ground pepper
Clarified Butter (see recipe) (optional)
Lemon wedges for garnish

Crush the juniper berries, and sprinkle them over both sides of the salmon steaks, pressing the berries into the flesh so they will adhere. Coat the fish with olive oil, and sprinkle with salt and pepper.

Grill over hot coals 4 minutes on each side, or until the fish flakes with a fork. Or pan-fry in clarified butter for approximately the same length of time.

Garnish with lemon wedges and serve.

Fillets of Salmon Four Seasons

SERVES 4

This recipe originated from The Four Seasons restaurant in New York City. My chef in Miami Beach has revised their original recipe, and I'll let you decide on the final results.

THE SAUCE

1 cup dry red wine
1 cup Fish Stock (see recipe) or clam juice
1 teaspoon cracked black peppercorns
3 shallots, finely diced
3 sprigs parsley
3 tablespoons finely chopped celery leaves
1 cup heavy cream

Four 8-ounce fillets (about 1 inch thick) fresh salmon, skinned

FOR THE MUSHROOMS

2 tablespoons olive oil
1/4 cup shallots, finely chopped
2 garlic cloves, finely chopped
1 1/2 pounds fresh wild mushrooms, such as chanterelles, shiitakes, or
*   morels*
Salt and freshly ground pepper to taste
1/2 cup fresh herbs, such as a combination of parsley, chives, dill, and
*   tarragon (if not all herbs available, use what you can get)*

Simmer the red wine, fish stock, cracked peppercorns, diced shallots, parsley, and celery leaves in a saucepan over low heat until reduced to ½ cup. Add the cream and simmer until reduced to 1 cup. Strain and keep warm in the top of a double boiler.

Steam the salmon fillets in a fish poacher or bamboo steamer for about 5 minutes.

Heat the olive oil in a skillet until it sizzles, add the chopped shallots and garlic and sauté for 1 minute only—*do not brown.* Add the mushrooms and cook over high heat until tender. Season with salt and pepper. Stir in the blended herbs.

To serve, divide the wine sauce on 4 serving plates. Place salmon fillets on top of the sauce, and top with mushrooms.

Salmon au Beaujolais

SERVES 4

1 large onion, finely chopped
½ cup butter
Salt and freshly ground pepper to taste
4 salmon steaks (about 8 ounces each)
3½ cups Beaujolais wine
1 bay leaf
6 sprigs parsley
2 garlic cloves, mashed
3 teaspoons all-purpose flour, blended with 4 tablespoons butter
4 tablespoons chopped chives

Sauté the onion in the butter. When the onion starts to brown, remove from the heat. Add salt and pepper. Place the onion in the bottom of a glass or ceramic baking dish large enough to accommodate all the steaks in one layer. Place salmon in the baking dish, and pour the wine over the fish. Add the bay leaf, parsley, and garlic, cover, and simmer on top of the stove about

10 to 12 minutes, or until the salmon is done. Remove the salmon to a warm platter.

Strain the wine sauce into a saucepan and bring to a boil. Remove from the heat and gradually add the flour mixture. Blend well, using a whisk. Bring to a boil and boil 1 minute. Taste and adjust the seasoning.

Sprinkle the salmon with chopped chives, and serve with the sauce on the side.

Fillet of Salmon and Asparagus in Puff Pastry with Watercress Sauce

SERVES 4

1 small salmon (approximately 3 pounds)
Salt and freshly ground pepper to taste
1 pound asparagus, trimmed
1 pound fresh sea scallops
2 eggs
3 cups heavy cream
1 pound Cream Puff Paste (see recipe), or store-bought
1 tablespoon water
3 tablespoons unsalted butter
4 medium shallots, chopped
1 bunch fresh watercress, chopped
1 cup dry white wine
Juice of 1 lemon, or to taste

Split the salmon in half, and bone and skin it. Season with salt and pepper. Reserve in the refrigerator.

In a large pot of boiling water, cook the asparagus until tender, about 5 to 7 minutes. Refresh them in ice-cold water, drain, and set aside.

To prepare the fish mousse, purée the scallops in a food

mill or food processor fitted with a steel blade. Add 1 egg, mix well, and, with the motor running, add 2 cups cream. Season with salt and pepper. Refrigerate immediately. To purée the scallops in a blender, you will need to work them in four or more batches.

Divide the pastry dough in half and roll out each piece approximately ⅛ inch thick into a rectangle larger than the fish. Place 1 piece of dough on a baking sheet. In the center, place half of the fish, spread with half the mousse, lay the asparagus on top, and spread with the remaining mousse. Top with the remaining salmon half.

Beat the remaining egg lightly with 1 tablespoon water to make an egg wash. Brush the pastry around the edge of the fish with the egg wash, then cover with the second sheet of pastry, pressing well around the fish to seal the edges. Trim the pastry, following the outline of the fish. Use any leftover dough to decorate the fish as you wish. Cover and chill in the refrigerator for 45 minutes

Preheat the oven to 400°F.

Uncover the fish and bake 35 to 45 minutes, until the pastry is golden brown and a knife inserted in the center of the fish for 1 minute feels hot to the lips.

While the fish is baking, prepare the sauce. In a saucepan over medium heat, melt 1 tablespoon butter. Sauté the chopped shallots and watercress until wilted. Deglaze pan with the wine, and reduce the sauce to ¼ cup. Add the remaining 1 cup cream and reduce until the sauce thickens. Slowly whisk in the remaining 2 tablespoons butter, 1 small piece at a time. In a blender or food processor, blend well for 1 minute, until smooth. Season with salt, pepper, and lemon juice to taste. Strain and keep warm.

With an electric or serrated knife, carefully slice the fish into 4 portions. Cover the bottom of each plate with the sauce and top with a slice of fish in pastry.

Gravlax with Dill-Mustard Sauce

SERVES 6 TO 8

Gravlax, or pickled salmon, is a Scandinavian method with an end result somewhere between lox and pickled herring fillets. We serve this in both restaurants with Dill-Mustard Sauce. You can use this as an appetizer, for a special occasion, or as a main course with onion slices, gherkins, and melba toast, but remember you must begin to cure the salmon 3 days in advance.

One 2-pound salmon fillet, boned, skin intact
2/3 cup sugar
1/3 cup salt
1 bunch fresh dill, separated into 3 bundles
2 tablespoons dill seed
Lemon wedges
Pumpernickel bread, thinly sliced
Dill-Mustard Sauce (see following recipe)

Cut the fillet crosswise into 2 large pieces. Combine the sugar and salt, and rub the mixture completely into the fish. Place 1 bundle of dill in the bottom of an enameled dish or glass bowl, then add 1 piece of salmon, skin side down. Sprinkle the fish with 1 tablespoon dill seed, and cover with a bundle of dill. Cover with the other piece of fillet, skin side up, sprinkle with the remaining 1 tablespoon dill seed, and top with the remaining bundle of fresh dill. Place a heavy plate or weight on top of the fish and leave in refrigerator for 3 days, turning twice a day and basting with the liquid that forms around the fish.

Before serving, scrape off all spices and cut the salmon into thin slices. Serve with lemon wedges, thinly sliced pumpernickel bread, and Dill-Mustard Sauce.

Dill-Mustard Sauce

MAKES ABOUT 3/4 CUP

3 tablespoons Dijon mustard
1 teaspoon dry mustard
2 tablespoons sugar
1 tablespoon red wine vinegar
1/3 cup vegetable oil
2 tablespoons chopped fresh dill

In a blender, combine all the ingredients except the dill. When the sauce thickens, stir in dill. Refrigerate 1 hour before serving.

Crab Imperial

SERVES 6 TO 8

A quick and easy version of our restaurant special—our guests are always asking for this recipe.

2 pounds fresh lump crabmeat
1 1/2 cups mayonnaise
2 tablespoons minced shallots or scallions
2 tablespoons chopped fresh parsley
3 eggs, lightly beaten
2 tablespoons Dijon mustard
Juice of 2 lemons
Salt and freshly ground white pepper to taste
1 pinch of ground cumin
2 teaspoons Worcestershire sauce

Preheat the oven to 400°F.

Place the crabmeat in a round-bottomed bowl. Blend the mayonnaise with all the remaining ingredients, stirring well. Add this mixture to the crabmeat and blend carefully to avoid breaking the lumps.

Gently spoon the crabmeat mixture into 8 individual baking shells or into a large shallow baking dish. The crabmeat mixture should be no more than 2 inches deep. Bake 10 to 12 minutes, or until done.

Soft-shell Crabs with Tomato Butter

SERVES 4

TOMATO BUTTER

4 medium ripe tomatoes, peeled, seeded, and chopped
1 cup heavy cream
1 cup unsalted butter, cut into small pieces
Salt and freshly ground pepper to taste
1 dash of cayenne
2 tablespoons minced fresh herbs such as chives or tarragon

SOFT-SHELL CRABS

12 live soft-shell crabs, cleaned
1/2 cup all-purpose flour
2 eggs, lightly beaten
2 cups fresh bread crumbs
4 tablespoons butter, or as needed

3 tablespoons capers, drained
3 tablespoons julienne of bacon, sautéed and drained

164

In a blender or in the work bowl of a food processor fitted with the steel blade, chop the tomatoes very finely. Strain the chopped tomatoes into a saucepan. Reduce over moderately high heat until it begins to thicken slightly. Add ¾ cup heavy cream and continue to reduce until the sauce thickens. Whisk in the butter, 1 piece at a time. Season with salt and pepper, a dash of cayenne, and the minced herbs. Set aside.

Rinse the live crabs carefully under cold running water. Put the flour on a plate. Dredge the crabs in the flour, dip them in the beaten eggs, and then in the bread crumbs to coat them well. Shake off any excess bread crumbs. Heat a large skillet over moderate heat and add 2 tablespoons butter. When the butter is hot and has stopped foaming, sauté the crabs, shell side down, for 5 to 6 minutes, or until they turn golden brown and crisp. Add more butter, if necessary. Turn the crabs and cook 5 minutes longer.

To serve, spoon the Tomato Butter on 4 plates, place 3 soft-shell crabs per plate on top of sauce, and sprinkle with the capers and sautéed bacon.

Charlotte of Crayfish in Cream of Vermouth

SERVES 4

60 large live crayfish
Plain Court Bouillon for Fish (see recipe)
4 trays of ice cubes (about 48 cubes)
1 small eggplant
Salt and freshly ground pepper to taste
2 medium zucchini
1 cup olive oil, or as needed
4 large tomatoes, peeled
1 cup dry vermouth
1 cup heavy cream
4 tablespoons butter
16 cherry tomatoes for garnish

Wash the crayfish under cold running water in a colander. Pour the court bouillon into a large pot, add the live crayfish, cover, and bring to a boil. Turn off the heat. Remove the crayfish with a strainer, reserving the liquid, and place them on a large plate. Cover them with the ice cubes. Separate 4 nice crayfish for a garnish, cover in a small bowl with ice cubes, and set aside. Take the remaining crayfish and crack them in half. Remove the tail meat, place on a plate, and keep covered in the refrigerator. Discard the shells and heads.

Clean and slice the eggplant into ¼-inch rounds, and season with salt and pepper. Clean and slice 1 zucchini into ¼-inch rounds, and season with salt and pepper. In a large skillet over medium-high heat, sauté the eggplant slices in 2 tablespoons olive oil until golden brown on both sides. Add more oil if necessary. Remove and drain on paper towels. Sauté the zucchini slices in the same skillet, in oil, until golden brown. Remove and drain on paper towels.

Cut the tomatoes into quarters, removing the stem from the top. Sauté the tomato quarters in 2 tablespoons olive oil in a medium saucepan over high heat, stirring vigorously with a fork to mash them as they cook. Boil for about 10 minutes, until they become a purée. Stir in salt and pepper to taste, and reserve.

Place 1 eggplant slice in each of four 8-ounce individual aluminum molds. Cover the eggplant with crayfish tails, and spread some tomato purée over the crayfish. Place a layer of zucchini slices over the tomato purée, overlapping the slices around in a circle. Cover the zucchini with another layer of crayfish, spread more tomato purée over the crayfish, and place 1 eggplant slice on top. Set the molds aside.

To prepare the sauce, strain the court bouillon and boil 2 cups until it is reduced by half. Add the vermouth and cook 5 minutes more. Add the heavy cream and boil until thick (about 5 minutes). Add the butter, season with salt and pepper, and whisk briskly until smooth and creamy. Cover and reserve.

In a vegetable steamer, steam the cherry tomatoes to soften them slightly. Cover and set aside.

Place the molds in a pan of simmering hot water for 10 minutes. While the crayfish molds are heating, cut the remaining zucchini into very thin strips and reserve.

Carefully turn the molds out onto 4 large dinner plates. Heat the sauce, and pour ⅓ cup over each charlotte. Garnish each serving with the zucchini strips, 1 reserved whole crayfish, and 4 cherry tomatoes. Serve at once.

Garlic-Broiled Shrimp

SERVES 6

A garlic-lover's delight, this dish is so easy to prepare you can make it and serve it to company after a full day's work! We serve it at dinner in Washington, D.C., with sautéed snow peas on the side.

4 pounds large raw shrimp, peeled, deveined, leaving on tails
½ cup unsalted butter
½ cup olive oil
4 scallions, chopped
4 large garlic cloves, minced
1½ tablespoons fresh lemon juice
1¼ teaspoons Worcestershire sauce
½ teaspoon Tabasco sauce
1 teaspoon salt
2 tablespoons minced fresh parsley, preferably flat-leaved
⅓ cup freshly grated Parmesan
Parsley sprigs for garnish

Divide the shrimp equally among 4 small gratin dishes and set aside. In a heavy 2-quart saucepan, heat the butter with the olive oil. Add all remaining ingredients, except the cheese and parsley sprigs, and cook 5 minutes over medium heat.

Position the broiler rack 4 inches below the source of heat and preheat.

Pour the garlic-butter sauce equally over the shrimp, then top with a generous sprinkling of Parmesan. Place the gratin dishes on a large baking sheet and broil until the shrimp are coral-pink and the sauce is bubbly and lightly browned, about 5 minutes. Serve hot, garnished with parsley sprigs.

Baked Bluefish with Vegetables

SERVES 4

Maybe the best bluefish you ever tasted, this is good in the summer when these fish are plentiful and very fresh. Fillets must not be older than a few hours!

4 tablespoons butter
1 large onion, very thinly sliced
1 large carrot, finely shredded
1 cup chopped celery leaves
1/2 cup dry white wine
4 bluefish fillets (about 6 to 8 ounces each)
Juice of 2 lemons
Salt and freshly ground pepper to taste
16 very large spinach leaves, cleaned, stems removed
1 cup watercress leaves
1/2 cup sliced mushrooms
3 large ripe tomatoes, thinly sliced
3 tablespoons chopped fresh parsley, or 2 tablespoons chopped fresh tarra-
  gon blended with 1 tablespoon chopped fresh parsley
4 tablespoons fresh bread crumbs

Preheat the oven to 425°F.

Heat the butter in a large flameproof baking dish. Add the onion, carrot, and celery leaves. Cook over medium heat 5 minutes. Add the wine and simmer 3 minutes more, stirring occasionally, until the vegetables are tender but not brown.

Sprinkle the fillets with lemon juice, and season with salt

and pepper. Wrap 4 spinach leaves around each fillet. The best way to do this is to steam the spinach leaves on top of the vegetable-wine mixture for 1 or 2 minutes, then fold the leaves around the fish and set aside.

Arrange the watercress over the vegetable-wine mixture. Place the wrapped fillets over the watercress, sprinkle with mushrooms, and top with tomato slices. Dust with chopped parsley and bread crumbs. Bake 20 minutes, or until the fish is tender.

Dolphin Fish with Red Wine Sauce

SERVES 4

This is a personal favorite, a recipe I cook when fishing in Key West.

2 pounds mahimahi fillet (dolphin fish)
8 tablespoons butter
1/2 cup chopped shallots or scallions
2 1/2 cups dry red wine
1 bay leaf
2 sprigs thyme, or 1/2 teaspoon dried
4 tablespoons plus 1/3 cup chopped fresh parsley
4 tablespoons chopped celery
1 1/3 cups Demi-glace or Brown Sauce (see recipe) or, if not available, use
*   fresh or canned beef stock*
Juice of 1 lemon or lime
Salt and freshly ground pepper to taste
2 tablespoons all-purpose flour
1 cup thinly sliced mushrooms (optional)

Preheat the oven to 425°F.

Place the fish in a greased baking pan. Melt 4 tablespoons

butter in a saucepan over medium heat. Add the shallots or scallions and cook 1 minute, but *do not brown.* Add the wine, bay leaf, thyme, 4 tablespoons parsley, and the celery. Bring to a boil, then reduce heat and simmer about 15 minutes, or until the wine mixture is reduced to ¾ cup. Strain, pressing down hard on the vegetables and herbs to extract their flavor. Discard the solids.

Return the wine mixture to the saucepan. Add the demi-glace or beef stock and bring to a boil and reduce the volume by half. Add the lemon or lime juice, ⅓ cup parsley, salt, and pepper. Stir and simmer 5 minutes.

Blend the remaining 4 tablespoons butter and the flour together well (this is a lighter version of beurre manié; see p. 90). Add to the sauce gradually, as you bring the sauce to a quick boil. Simmer for 1 minute. Taste and adjust the seasoning. Add the thinly sliced mushrooms to the sauce, if you wish. Let the mushrooms simmer 2 minutes in the sauce.

Pour the sauce on top of the fish and bake about 10 minutes, or until tender.

Oven-Baked Monkfish

SERVES 4

This goes well with a side dish of boiled new potatoes

1 tablespoon olive oil
2 pounds monkfish fillets
Salt and freshly ground pepper to taste
6 anchovies, rinsed in cold water and drained on paper towels (see Note, p. 4)
2 cups heavy cream
2 tablespoons chopped fresh dill for garnish
2 tablespoons chopped fresh parsley for garnish

Preheat the oven to 375°F.

Brush a baking dish with the olive oil. Sprinkle the fish with salt and pepper, and lay the fillets on the bottom of the dish in a single layer. Mash the anchovies into a paste, and gradually blend in the cream. Pour the anchovy-cream mixture over the fish. Place, uncovered, in the oven and bake 15 to 20 minutes, or until the fish is tender. Remove from the oven and sprinkle with dill and parsley.

Shark with Mozzarella Cheese

SERVES 4

Mako shark, caught off the coast of Long Island, is the best shark in the United States for eating. Serve with green vegetables or mushrooms of your choice.

2 pounds shark fillets or chunks
Salt and freshly ground pepper to taste
1 1/2 cups sour cream
2/3 cup diced onion
1/3 cup diced scallions (use green tops only)
4 garlic cloves, thinly sliced
1 cup shredded mozzarella cheese
1/3 cup finely chopped fresh parsley or chives for garnish

Preheat the oven to 325°F.

Cut the fish into serving portions. Place in one layer in a well-buttered shallow baking pan. Sprinkle with salt and pepper. Combine the sour cream, onion, scallion, and garlic, and spread this sauce over the fish. Sprinkle with mozzarella, and bake 25 to 30 minutes, or until the fish is tender and the cheese lightly browned. Sprinkle with parsley or chives.

171

Broiled Mako
à la Dominique

SERVES 4

Two 1-inch-thick mako steaks (8 ounces each)
Juice of 2 lemons
1 teaspoon minced fresh garlic
1 teaspoon dried oregano
1 teaspoon finely chopped fresh dill
4 tablespoons butter, melted
Salt and freshly ground pepper to taste

Place the mako in a shallow glass dish. Squeeze the lemon juice over the fish, turning to coat both sides. Sprinkle with garlic, oregano, and dill. Marinate in the refrigerator 45 minutes, turning every 15 minutes.

Adjust your broiler rack so that the fish will be 4 inches below the source of heat. (You can also prepare this on a charcoal grill. Adjust the rack accordingly.) Preheat the broiler 10 minutes.

Place the steaks on a lightly oiled rack, reserving the marinade. Brush with melted butter. A 1-inch-thick steak should be broiled (or grilled) approximately 10 minutes (5 minutes per side). When the steaks are turned, brush with melted butter, and baste often with the marinade. Since the flesh is always meaty and firm, you'll find it doesn't crumble when turned with a wide spatula. Broil until the surface is very lightly browned. Season with salt and pepper. You can dress this dish with Hollandaise Sauce (see recipe), tartar sauce, or melted butter.

Baked Stuffed Trout

SERVES 4

4 whole trout (8 to 10 ounces each), gutted and cleaned
Salt and freshly ground pepper to taste
Crabmeat Stuffing for Fish (see following recipe)
4 tablespoons unsalted butter, melted
2 cups dry white wine
1/2 cup Fish Stock (see recipe) or clam juice
1 tablespoon fresh lemon juice
1/2 cup finely chopped onion
1/2 cup finely chopped celery leaves
1 cup finely chopped fresh parsley
1 bay leaf
1 sprig thyme, or 1/2 teaspoon dried

Preheat the oven to 425°F.

Rinse the trout in cold water and pat dry. Season each fish with salt and pepper, and stuff with the stuffing. Brush a baking pan with 2 tablespoons melted butter and place the fish in the pan. Add the remaining melted butter, wine, fish stock, lemon juice, onion, celery leaves, 1/2 cup chopped parsley, bay leaf, and thyme. Bake about 30 minutes, or until the fish is tender. Remove the fish from the oven and place on a heated serving platter. Remove and discard bay leaf.

Strain the juice from the pan. Return to the pan and boil over high heat, reducing it by half. Pour the hot juice over the stuffed fish. Sprinkle with the remaining 1/2 cup parsley, and serve at once.

Crabmeat Stuffing for Fish

MAKES ABOUT 1 CUP

This stuffing is quite tasty and can be used for any fish of your choice. The quantity can be increased for stuffing larger fish.

³/₈ pound fresh fish fillets, such as Boston sole, halibut, or sea trout
1 teaspoon finely chopped shallots
1 ¹/₂ teaspoons finely chopped fresh parsley
1 egg white
1 ¹/₂ tablespoons heavy cream
Salt and freshly ground pepper to taste
³/₈ cup fresh lump crabmeat

Combine the fish fillets with the shallots and parsley in a blender, food mill, or food processor. Purée until creamy, then add the egg white and process to blend well. Add the heavy cream, salt, and pepper, and blend again. Place this mixture in a bowl and gently fold in the crabmeat.

Baked Red Snapper in Ratatouille

SERVES 6

1/3 cup olive oil
4 large onions, sliced
4 green peppers, seeded and cut into strips
3/4 pound eggplant, sliced
4 garlic cloves, crushed
1 1/2 pounds tomatoes, peeled, seeded, and chopped
Salt and freshly ground pepper to taste
3/4 pound zucchini, sliced
6 tablespoons chopped fresh parsley
4 sprigs tarragon, or 2 teaspoons dried
1 red snapper fillet (about 3 pounds)
8 garlic cloves, cut in slivers
1 bay leaf for garnish
Lemon wedges for garnish

Preheat the oven to 375°F.

In a large saucepan, heat the oil and sauté the onions until tender. Add the green peppers and cook until soft. Add the eggplant, crushed garlic, tomatoes, salt, and pepper. Cook over medium heat to reduce and thicken the ratatouille. Add the zucchini and continue cooking until almost all liquid has evaporated. Taste and adjust the seasoning. Sprinkle with parsley and half the tarragon, and set aside.

Stud the red snapper fillet with slivers of garlic, inserting them evenly over the entire fillet. Place the ratatouille in a baking dish, and lay the fish on top. Cook about 25 minutes, or until done, turning the fish once during baking. Remove the garlic slivers from the fish and discard. Add the remaining tarragon and bay leaf as garnishes, and serve with lemon wedges.

Grouper or Snapper Creole

SERVES 4

2 *tablespoons butter*
1 *cup chopped Spanish onions*
2 *tablespoons chopped shallots or scallions*
2 *garlic cloves, crushed*
4 *cups peeled, seeded, and chopped ripe tomatoes or drained canned Italian*
    tomatoes
1 *cup dry white wine*
1 *tablespoon dried thyme*
2 *tablespoons fresh basil, or* 1/2 *teaspoon dried*
1 *teaspoon salt*
Freshly ground pepper to taste
1 *tablespoon red wine vinegar*
2 *cups finely chopped green pepper*
1 *cup finely chopped red pepper*
4 *grouper or snapper fillets (about 8 ounces each)*
8 *lemon slices*
1/3 *cup chopped fresh parsley*
4 *tablespoons grated Parmesan*

Melt the butter in a large saucepan, and add the onions, shallots or scallions, and garlic. Cook until tender, but do not brown. Add the tomatoes, wine, thyme, basil, salt, pepper, vinegar, and green and red peppers. Reduce the heat and simmer 15 minutes.

As soon as the peppers are tender, add the fish. Cover the pan and continue cooking about 8 minutes, or until the fish is done.

Remove the fish to a warm platter and top with sauce. Arrange 2 lemon slices over each fillet, sprinkle with parsley and Parmesan, and serve at once.

Snook or Red Snapper, Key West Style

SERVES 4

I make this at home in Key West with snook that I catch myself. If you can't find snook, substitute red snapper.

4 snook or red snapper fillets (about 8 ounces each)
4 tablespoons olive oil
1 cup chopped Spanish onions
1/3 cup chopped celery
4 cups drained canned Italian tomatoes or peeled, seeded, and chopped ripe
   tomatoes
1 teaspoon salt
1/2 teaspoon pepper
2 dashes of Tabasco sauce
6 chopped fresh basil leaves, or 1 1/2 teaspoons dried
2 tablespoons capers, chopped
8 lime slices
1/2 cup chopped fresh parsley for garnish

Rinse the fillets in cold water, pat dry, and set aside. Heat the olive oil in a skillet and sauté the onions and celery until tender. Add the tomatoes, salt, pepper, Tabasco, basil, and capers. Cover the pan partially and simmer very slowly 15 minutes, or until the sauce is reduced to 1 cup.

Place the fish fillets on top of sauce, cover the pan, and cook slowly, about 3 minutes on each side, or until the fish is done. Arrange 2 lime slices on top of each cooked fillet. Remove the fish to a warmed platter and spoon the sauce over the fish. Sprinkle with parsley and serve immediately.

Fillets of Rockfish Provençal

SERVES 4

At Dominique's in Miami Beach, we serve this with Spinach Flan (see recipe) as a garniture. This recipe is also good made with bluefish, which is plentiful in the summer.

4 fresh rockfish fillets (about 8 to 10 ounces each)
Salt and freshly ground pepper to taste
1/2 cup all-purpose flour
1/2 cup vegetable oil
2 lemons, halved
6 tablespoons butter
2 tablespoons finely chopped shallots or scallions
1/2 cup finely chopped celery leaves
4 garlic cloves, crushed
2 1/2 cups peeled, seeded, and chopped ripe tomatoes or drained canned
*   tomatoes*
3 tablespoons finely chopped herbs, such as parsley, tarragon, or dill

Preheat the oven to 425°F.

Rinse the fish fillets in cold water and pat dry. Season with salt and pepper, and roll in the flour, shaking off the excess. Heat the oil in a skillet, add the fillets, and sauté on both sides until golden brown. Remove the fillets to a baking pan, squeezing fresh lemon juice over them. Discard the cooking oil.

In the same skillet, melt the butter over medium heat. Add the shallots or scallions, celery leaves, and garlic. Cook 1 minute, stirring constantly. *Do not brown.* Add the tomatoes, bring to a boil, and continue cooking over medium heat until the mixture is reduced to 1 cup, about 10 minutes.

Pour the tomato sauce over fish, and bake 5 minutes, or until very hot. Remove from the oven, remove and discard the garlic, and sprinkle with herbs of your choice. Serve immediately.

Fried Fish,
Mexican Style

SERVES 4

This is a good recipe, very nice and easy to make.

4 garlic cloves, peeled
Vegetable oil for frying
4 whole fish (about 1 pound each), such as sea bass or snapper, scaled and
    cleaned, with heads removed
1 cup sifted all-purpose flour
1 tablespoon salt
4 fresh limes

Place the garlic in a frying kettle with about 1 ½ inches oil and heat the oil to 375°F. When the garlic is toasted golden brown, remove and discard it.

Score each fish by making diagonal cuts on both sides with a sharp knife. Coat the fish with flour and salt, shaking off any excess. Cook the fish in the preheated oil flavored with garlic until golden brown on both sides, approximately 10 minutes on each side, turning once. The fish should flake easily with a fork. Drain briefly on paper towels.

Place the fish on a serving plate. Squeeze the juice of 2 limes over the fish, then surround with the remaining 2 limes cut into wedges.

Mustard-Fried Fish

SERVES 4

Four 8-ounce fish fillets, such as snapper, mahimahi, catfish, grouper,
*   cobia, or sea bass*
1 cup vegetable oil for frying
1 1/2 cups mild prepared yellow mustard
2 eggs, well beaten with a fork
1 teaspoon Tabasco sauce
1 1/2 cups yellow cornmeal
1/2 cup all-purpose flour
1 cup Italian-seasoned bread crumbs
2 teaspoons salt
1 teaspoon freshly ground pepper
1 1/2 teaspoons Hungarian paprika
Lemon wedges
Tartar sauce

Rinse the fish and pat dry with paper towels, then set aside. In a heavy 12-inch cast-iron skillet, heat the oil until it sizzles.

While the oil is heating, combine the mustard, eggs, and Tabasco in a flat dish or shallow bowl, stirring to combine well. In a separate shallow pan or bowl, combine the cornmeal, flour, bread crumbs, salt, pepper, and paprika and stir to blend. Dip the fish into the egg-mustard mixture, then dredge in the corn-meal-crumb mixture, turning to coat all surfaces. Shake off the excess. Gently place the fish in the preheated oil and fry until golden brown and crispy, 4 to 5 minutes on each side, turning once. Drain on paper towels, and serve with lemon wedges, tartar sauce, and Creamy Coleslaw (see recipe).

Eel Matelote

SERVES 4

This is a European favorite that has become a Dominique's favorite in both Miami Beach and Washington, D.C.

2 pounds eel, cleaned and skinned, head and tail removed
18 small white onions, peeled
1 large carrot, thinly sliced
1³/4 cups dry red wine
1 cup Chicken Stock (see recipe)
2 bay leaves
1 sprig thyme, or ¹/4 teaspoon dried
1 garlic clove, minced
3 tablespoons butter
2 tablespoons all-purpose flour
¹/2 cup light cream
Salt and freshly ground pepper to taste
2 tablespoons chopped fresh chives for garnish

Cut the eel into 3-inch lengths, and wipe dry. In a deep pan, combine the onions, carrot, wine, chicken stock, bay leaves, thyme, and garlic. Bring to a quick boil, then reduce heat and simmer 15 minutes. Add the eel and simmer an additional 20 minutes, or until the fish is tender. Remove the eel and vegetables and place on a warm serving platter. Discard the bay leaves. Strain the red wine sauce, and set aside.

Melt the butter in a saucepan over medium heat. Stir in the flour and cook 2 minutes, stirring, without browning the flour. Remove from the heat and add the cream and reserved red wine sauce, stirring constantly. Cook over medium heat 15 minutes. Season with salt and pepper.

Pour the sauce over the fish and vegetables, and sprinkle with fresh chives. Serve with toasted French bread.

Pompano en Papillote

SERVES 4

For variety, try this preparation with fillets of red snapper, sea bass, flounder, or red salmon. Fillets should be no more than ¾ inch thick. The classic shape for preparations *en papillote* is heart shaped. The fish is placed on one side of the heart along with the other ingredients. The empty side of the heart is folded over the fish, and the edges are rolled up tightly to make the cooking package.

2 carrots, finely cut into julienne strips
4 shallots, finely chopped
½ cup finely chopped celery leaves
⅓ cup chopped fresh parsley
1 cup finely chopped mushrooms
3 tablespoons dry white wine or Fish Stock (see recipe)
6 tablespoons butter, at room temperature
4 pompano fillets (about 8 ounces each)
Salt and freshly ground pepper to taste
Lemon wedges for garnish

Preheat the oven to 400°F.

Combine all of the vegetables in a bowl, add the wine or fish stock, and mix well.

Use about 2 tablespoons butter to grease the 4 pieces of heart-shaped baking parchment. Place each fish fillet on the left half of the parchment heart. Season with salt and pepper. Divide the vegetable mixture evenly into 4 portions and place on top of each fish fillet. Sprinkle with more salt and pepper and dot each with 1 tablespoon butter. Fold the right half of the parchment heart over the filling and fold up the edges, crimping securely.

Bake until the paper is browned and puffed, about 7 to 9 minutes. Serve with lemon wedges, and cut open the paper at the table.

Steamed Fish,
Cantonese Style

SERVES 4, DEPENDING ON SIZE OF FISH

Robert F. P. Tsui of the Peking Gourmet Inn in Falls Church, Virginia, recently gave me this recipe. Steamed fish is one of my favorite foods, and the Peking Gourmet Inn cooks it perfectly.

Cantonese steamed fish is a simple preparation that must be accurate; the fish must be steamed *to the exact moment* when the meat flakes off from the central bones. Robert says this takes either "a lot of experience or a lot of luck."

1 1/2 to 2 1/2 pounds whole flounder, sea bass, or snapper, cleaned and scaled, with head and tail intact
Salt to taste
About 16 pieces fresh ginger, peeled and thinly sliced
1/2 cup scallions, trimmed and julienned
3 ounces peanut or soya oil

After the general cleaning of the fish, sprinkle with salt and set aside for 3 minutes. Then rinse in a bowl of cold water and pat dry with paper towels. Slice the sides of the fish diagonally, just partway through the flesh, and insert ginger slices in the cuts (about 4 cuts per side, depending on the size of the fish). Scatter half the julienned scallions on top of the fish, and steam in a tightly closed steamer until done, about 10 minutes for a 1 1/2-pound fish.

Remove the fish from the steamer and discard the ginger pieces and scallions. Insert fresh ginger slices into the fish, and set on a platter. Scatter with fresh julienned scallions. Heat the oil to smoking, then drizzle over fish and serve.

Fresh Tuna in Lettuce

SERVES 4

This recipe also works well with salmon and swordfish.

4 tuna steaks (about 1 1/4 inches thick, about 8 ounces each)
Juice of 4 lemons (optional)
1 Spanish onion, thinly sliced
1/2 cup diced celery
1/4 cup olive oil
4 anchovy fillets, rinsed in cold water and finely chopped
2 tablespoons chopped fresh dill or tarragon
Salt and freshly ground pepper to taste
8 large leaves Boston lettuce, blanched in boiling water for 1 minute and
*   drained*
2 tablespoons butter
1 1/3 cups dry white wine
1/2 cup chopped watercress
4 lemon wedges for garnish

Steam the fish in a steamer for 2 to 3 minutes or, if no steamer is available, poach in boiling water to cover. If poaching the fish, squeeze lemon juice into the water before adding fish; simmer 2 minutes. Discard the water and reserve the fish.

In a skillet over medium-high heat, cook the onion and celery in the oil. When the oil is sizzling, place the steaks in the pan, lower the heat, and brown the fish slowly. Do not brown the onions. Turn the fish over and spread the chopped anchovies and dill or tarragon on top. Season with salt and pepper.

Remove the fish from the pan and wrap each steak tightly and entirely in 2 lettuce leaves. Put the wrapped fish back into the skillet, cover, and cook, gradually adding the butter and wine. Allow the fish to simmer 20 to 25 minutes, or until done.

Place the wrapped fish on a deep serving platter, and top with the pan juices and vegetables. Sprinkle with watercress, and serve with lemon wedges.

Game
and Other
Exotica

The United States is extremely rich in wildlife, but here game is not always considered the delicacy it is in Europe and other parts of the world. This picture is changing, however, with the heightened interest in gourmet cuisine and an insistence on quality, freshness, and originality in the foods we eat.

If you buy your game, buy it from a reliable source. And be certain that you are getting what you pay for. (A note of warning: In some states, alligators are protected by the federal government, so check with your local wildlife agency before killing or purchasing any.) Our alligator dishes are enjoyed both in Miami Beach and Washington, D.C.—so much so that I've included some of the favorites for you to cook at home. But, out of the entire animal, the only really good cut of meat is from the center cut of the tail. So when you buy your alligator steaks to prepare these recipes, be sure to insist on fillets cut from the center section of the tail.

I have spent many days hunting and fishing, in the wind and the rain, under a scorching-hot sun, in cold ice and snow—all experiences that I remember fondly. However, as any hunter will tell you, the chief satisfaction of hunting is *not* in the quick act of killing, but in the company of friends, in the act of trekking through the woods and watching the sun rise or set beyond a river or stream. And for me, the greatest reward of all comes even later, as I transform these creatures into delectable dishes and sit down with my friends to enjoy the good taste of wild game with a good bottle of wine.

There are a few points you should remember when handling wild game yourself:

- If the game has been damaged by shots, cut away the damaged area and the area immediately surrounding it.

- Dress the meat immediately, that is, remove all viscera, hair, and blood, and clean off all dirt.

- Cover the meat with cheesecloth to keep it free of dirt, bugs, and flies.

- Meat should be cooled as soon as possible, preferably by hanging the game in a cool room with plenty of air circulation. Meat should remain at about 40°F. from 2 days to a week, depending on the size of the animal. The longer meat is allowed to age, the more tender it becomes.

- Game meat can be ruined by improper butchering; if you don't know how, ask a professional butcher or cook to do the job.

We raise the game for Dominique's on my farm in Maryland, and it is very popular on our restaurant menus. I've included in this section some recipes I make myself when I'm at the farm, along with the dishes all our guests enjoy at Dominique's.

Casserole of Pheasant

SERVES 2

This recipe can be doubled easily and successfully to serve 4. Serve with Red Cabbage (see recipe) and peeled, sliced apples sautéed in butter.

2 young pheasants (about 2 pounds each), or 1 large pheasant (about 4
 to 5 pounds), well cleaned and rinsed
3 tablespoons butter
3 tablespoons vegetable oil
1 large onion, finely sliced
3 tablespoons all-purpose flour
2 cups Chicken Stock (see recipe), or more as needed
1 large carrot, thinly sliced
1 celery stalk with leaves, thinly sliced
1 1/2 cups dry red or white wine
1 bay leaf
10 sprigs parsley, chopped
1 sprig thyme, or 1/8 teaspoon dried
Salt and freshly ground pepper to taste
1/3 cup light cream
1 cup small mushrooms, cleaned and trimmed

Preheat the oven to 375°F.

 Cut each pheasant into 8 serving pieces, discarding the backbone. Heat the butter and oil over high heat in a large skillet until sizzling, then reduce the heat, add the pheasant pieces, and sauté until evenly browned and golden. Remove the meat from the skillet and place in a casserole.

 Add the onion to the skillet and sauté over medium heat until tender but not browned. Stir in the flour and cook over low heat, stirring, until the flour and onions start to brown, about 10 minutes. Gradually add the chicken stock, blending well with a wire whisk. Bring to a boil, stirring constantly, and remove

187

from the heat as soon as the sauce thickens. Add the sliced carrot, celery, wine, bay leaf, parsley, thyme, salt, and pepper, return to the heat, and simmer gently 15 minutes. The sauce should have the consistency of light cream, and all the ingredients should be well blended. If the sauce is too thick, thin with a little chicken stock, then simmer a bit longer to reduce.

Pour the wine sauce over the pheasant in the casserole, cover, and bake 1 hour and 10 minutes. Remove from the oven, remove and discard the bay leaf, then stir in the cream and mushrooms. Blend well, and taste and adjust the seasoning. Return the casserole to the oven and bake 10 minutes more.

Roasted Pheasant with Mushrooms and Madeira Sauce

SERVES 2

This elegant dish will dress up any occasion. The recipe can be doubled to serve 4.

1 medium pheasant (about 3 to 4 pounds), well cleaned
Salt and freshly ground pepper to taste
1 Spanish onion, sliced
1 large carrot, sliced
2 sprigs thyme
6 tablespoons Clarified Butter (see recipe)
2 tablespoons vegetable oil
3/4 cup Chicken Stock (see recipe)
1/3 cup Madeira
1/2 cup heavy cream
2 tablespoons unsalted butter
4 tablespoons chopped shallots
2 cups chopped fresh domestic or wild mushrooms, cleaned and trimmed
3 teaspoons green peppercorns
4 tablespoons chopped fresh parsley

Sprinkle the pheasant inside and out with salt and pepper. In a small bowl, combine the onion, carrot, and thyme, then stuff this mixture into the cavity of the bird. Set aside surplus vegetables, if any.

In a deep skillet, heat 4 tablespoons clarified butter, then add the oil. When sizzling, add the pheasant and sauté, turning from time to time, until evenly browned all over. Remove the bird from the skillet and set in a roasting pan. Add any reserved vegetables and about 3 tablespoons of the fat in the skillet, 2 tablespoons chicken stock, and 3 tablespoons Madeira to the roasting pan. Cover the pan and cook gently on top of the stove over medium heat for 30 to 45 minutes for rare or medium meat, basting and turning the pheasant occasionally.

While the pheasant is roasting, prepare the mushrooms and sauce. For the sauce, discard the remaining fat from the skillet in which you browned the pheasant. Add the remaining chicken stock and Madeira to the skillet and bring to a boil, stirring and scraping the bottom of the pan. Simmer and reduce to ½ cup. While the wine sauce is reducing, bring the cream to a boil in a separate pan and simmer to reduce by half. This should take about 10 minutes. Add the reduced cream to the reduced Madeira sauce, blend, and season to taste with salt and pepper. Strain, and let cool to lukewarm. Stir in the unsalted butter.

For the mushrooms, heat the remaining 2 tablespoons clarified butter in a clean skillet. When the butter sizzles, add the shallots and cook until tender. Add the mushrooms, peppercorns, salt, and pepper, and cook over high heat for 5 minutes, or until just tender. Sprinkle with chopped parsley, and taste and adjust the seasoning.

When the pheasant is cooked to the desired doneness, remove the bird to a warm platter. Drain the juice from the pan and add the mushrooms to the vegetables in the pan. Heat, stirring, to warm. Reheat the Madeira sauce, if necessary. To serve, carve the bird into 4 pieces, serve with the mushroom-vegetable mixture, and pass the Madeira sauce in a sauceboat at the table.

Quail en Papillote
with Julienne of Mushrooms

SERVES 4

8 boneless quail
Salt and freshly ground pepper to taste
About ¹/₂ cup olive oil
1 pound fresh shiitake mushrooms
11 tablespoons unsalted butter
2 teaspoons finely chopped shallots
¹/₂ cup dry white wine or dry vermouth

Season the quail with salt and pepper. In a large skillet, sauté the quail in ¼ cup olive oil over high heat for 2 minutes on each side, until golden brown. They should be only half-cooked. Remove them from the skillet, place on a large plate, cover, and set aside. Discard the oil.

Trim the shiitake mushrooms and discard the stems. Melt 2 tablespoons butter in a skillet over medium-high heat. When the butter is hot, add the mushrooms and sauté 5 to 8 minutes, stirring constantly. Remove from the skillet and set aside to cool. Slice the mushrooms lengthwise in ¼-inch julienne slices, and reserve.

Preheat the oven to 350°F.

Sauté the shallots in a skillet in 1 tablespoon butter until tender. Add the sliced mushrooms, sauté for 2 more minutes, and remove from the skillet and reserve.

Cut 4 circles of parchment paper of approximately 12 inches in diameter. Divide the mushroom-shallot mixture into equal portions and place on one side of each circle. For each parchment circle, place 2 quail on top of the mushrooms and shallots, and top with 2 tablespoons butter and 2 tablespoons wine or vermouth. Fold the parchment paper over the quail so that the edges meet. Fold the edges together tightly around the curved edge, sealing the *papillotes.* Brush the *papillotes* with the remaining ¼ cup olive oil to help the paper brown. Place the *papillotes* on a baking sheet and bake 10 minutes, or until done.

Remove the *papillotes* from the oven, slit open, and remove the tender quail, shiitake mushrooms, and shallots. Place each portion on a dinner plate, and pour the remaining juices over the top. Serve immediately.

Dove or Quail au Chablis with Garlic Toast

SERVES 4

Dominique's guests enjoy all our quail dishes. Even Warren Beatty has eaten quail in our Washington, D.C., restaurant. This recipe is a Dominique's favorite. We like to serve it with a garniture of Fried Grapes (see recipe).

8 whole doves or quail
⅓ cup vegetable oil
6 tablespoons all-purpose flour, seasoned with salt and pepper
⅓ cup butter
24 small mushrooms, cleaned, stemmed, and halved
½ cup Chablis or other dry white wine
¼ cup chopped fresh parsley
¼ cup chopped celery leaves

GARLIC TOAST

3 garlic cloves
⅓ cup plus 1½ tablespoons olive oil
4 slices French bread, sliced on the diagonal
⅓ cup butter

Rinse the birds under cold water and pat dry with paper towels. Brush the skin lightly with a little bit of the oil. Place the seasoned flour in a paper bag, add the birds, and shake to coat evenly. Heat the remaining oil in a large skillet and, when hot, add the birds and sauté 5 minutes, or until evenly browned. Remove the birds and discard the oil.

In the same skillet, melt the butter and add the mushrooms and wine. Bring to a quick boil, add the birds, parsley, and celery leaves; cover and simmer 30 minutes, or until done.

While the birds are cooking, prepare the garlic toast. Crush the garlic cloves, and mix with 1 ½ tablespoons olive oil. Spread this mixture on one side only of the French bread slices. Set aside for 5 minutes. Heat the remaining ⅓ cup olive oil and the butter in a skillet large enough to hold the bread slices in a single layer. Fry the bread, garlic side up.

When the birds are done, arrange them on top of the garlic toast. Strain the sauce in skillet, and spoon it over the birds.

Rabbit with Apples

SERVES 4

¼ pound salt pork, parboiled and diced, or ½ pound lean bacon
2 large onions, sliced
½ cup chopped celery
1 young rabbit, skinned and cleaned (head, tail, and feet removed), cut
*   into 8 serving pieces, liver and kidney reserved*
2 tablespoons all-purpose flour
2½ cups dry white wine
1 cup Chicken Stock (see recipe)
Salt and freshly ground pepper
1 bouquet garni (see p. 32)
2 cups peeled, cored, and sliced tart apples
3 tablespoons red wine vinegar
¼ cup sugar
1 cup chopped mushrooms

Fry the salt pork or bacon in a large skillet until golden brown. Remove from the skillet with a slotted spoon and place in a Dutch oven or stovetop casserole. Add the onions and celery to the skillet and cook in rendered fat over medium-high heat until tender. Add the vegetables to the casserole.

Dust the rabbit pieces with flour. Sauté the rabbit in the same skillet, turning the pieces from time to time to brown evenly. Place the browned meat on top of the salt pork or bacon and vegetables; add the wine, chicken stock, salt, pepper, and bouquet garni to the casserole. Chop the reserved liver and kidney, and add to the casserole.

Place casserole over high heat and bring to a boil. Reduce heat, cover, and simmer gently for 1 ½ hours, or until the rabbit is tender. Add the apple slices and simmer 8 minutes longer. In a small saucepan, combine the vinegar and sugar over high heat until the mixture turns golden and starts to carmelize. Stir quickly into the casserole, blending well. Remove and discard bouquet garni. Add the mushrooms, simmer 5 minutes more, and serve.

Rabbit in Wine Sauce

SERVES 4

1 large rabbit, skinned and cleaned (head, tail, and feet removed), cut into
    8 serving pieces
½ cup all-purpose flour, seasoned with salt and pepper
3 tablespoons olive oil
2 tablespoons butter, or more as needed
12 small boiling onions, peeled
6 garlic cloves, minced
1 bay leaf
1 sprig thyme, or ¼ teaspoon dried
1 branch rosemary, or 1 pinch dried
8 large mushrooms, cleaned and quartered
1 ¼ cups dry red wine
1 cup Beef Stock (see recipe)
1 ½ tablespoons cornstarch, dissolved in ¼ cup water
1 cup sour cream

Dust the rabbit pieces with seasoned flour. Heat the oil and butter in a heavy skillet, add the rabbit and sauté, turning often to brown evenly. Set the meat aside. In the same skillet, cook the onions until tender and barely browned. Add the garlic, bay leaf, thyme, rosemary, and mushrooms, adding more butter if needed. Cook 2 minutes over medium heat. Add the wine and beef stock and bring to a boil. Simmer gently 1 minute, then add the rabbit pieces, cover, and simmer 45 minutes, or until the meat is tender.

Remove the meat to a warm platter, and remove bay leaf and discard. Stir the dissolved cornstarch into the sauce and bring to a boil. Remove the skillet from the heat, add the sour cream, and stir well to blend. Return the pan to the heat and simmer, but *do not boil.* Taste and adjust the seasoning, then spoon the sauce over the rabbit pieces, and serve immediately.

Rabbit with Pernod

SERVES 4

Mashed potatoes make a great side dish with this.

1 rabbit, skinned and cleaned (head, tail, and feet removed) and cut into
    8 serving pieces
⅓ cup Pernod
1 tablespoon butter
3 tablespoons olive oil
12 small white onions, peeled
1 bouquet garni (see p. 32)
4 garlic cloves, crushed
½ cup pitted green olives
⅓ cup pitted black olives
1 bottle dry white wine
1 cup Beef Stock (see recipe)
4 large ripe tomatoes, peeled and seeded
⅓ cup salt pork, cut into strips
Salt and freshly ground pepper to taste
Chopped fresh parsley for garnish

Rub rabbit pieces with 1 tablespoon Pernod. In a large, heavy skillet, melt the butter over medium heat. Add the oil. When butter and oil begin to sizzle, add the rabbit pieces and brown evenly. Add the onions, bouquet garni, and garlic. Reduce heat, cover, and simmer gently about 45 minutes, stirring occasionally. Add olives.

Add the remaining Pernod and ignite. When the flame dies down, add the white wine, beef stock, tomatoes, salt pork, salt, and pepper. Simmer, uncovered, over medium heat 15 minutes or until tender. Remove salt pork and bouquet garni and discard. Sprinkle with parsley. Serve immediately with pan juices.

Marinated Roasted Venison

SERVES 8

The venison must marinate for 48 hours before cooking.

FOR THE MARINADE

2 large onions, thinly sliced
2 large carrots, sliced
1 celery stalk, sliced
8 sprigs parsley, chopped
2 sprigs thyme, or ½ teaspoon dried thyme
1 bay leaf
3 garlic cloves, crushed
2 whole cloves
3 cups dry red wine
1 cup red wine vinegar
½ cup water
4 tablespoons vegetable or peanut oil
Juice of 2 lemons
6 peppercorns

5 to 6 pounds venison meat, skinned, with nerves and membranes removed
   (leg, saddle, or other large piece)
Salt and freshly ground pepper to taste
½ cup melted butter
Sour Cream Sauce for Game (see following recipe) or Red Wine Sauce with
   Thyme (see recipe)

Combine all the marinade ingredients in a large saucepan and simmer 20 minutes. Cool to room temperature. Season the meat with salt and pepper, place in a deep pan, then pour the cooled marinade over the meat. Cover and refrigerate 48 hours, turning occasionally to marinate well.

   Preheat the oven to 450°F.

Remove the venison from the pan. Pour half the marinade and all the vegetables into a roasting pan. Place the meat on top. Brush the venison with melted butter, and roast 30 minutes. Lower the heat to 350°F. and roast 10 minutes per pound, or until the meat is cooked to your preference. Baste the meat frequently with the remaining marinade, and turn occasionally while roasting.

Carve the roasted venison and serve with Sour Cream Sauce for Game or Red Wine Sauce with Thyme.

Sour Cream Sauce for Game

MAKES 1 1/2 CUPS

3/4 cup dry red wine
1 tablespoon Cognac or brandy
1 teaspoon Worcestershire sauce
1/3 cup currant jelly
1 teaspoon all-purpose flour
1/2 cup sour cream
1 tablespoon melted butter
1/2 cup cooked sliced mushrooms (optional)
Salt and freshly ground pepper to taste

Boil the red wine, reducing it to ½ cup. Remove from the heat and add the Cognac, Worcestershire, and currant jelly, stirring rapidly to blend all the ingredients. Stir the flour into the sour cream, then add to the wine sauce. Return the pan to the heat and cook until the sauce thickens, but *do not boil.* Remove from the heat and stir in the melted butter and mushrooms, if desired. Taste and adjust the seasoning.

Roasted Leg of Venison
à la Moutarde

SERVES 6

This is a great hunting-lodge recipe, easy to make and good eaten cold the next day (if there are any leftovers) with an herb mayonnaise. Slice this roast very thin, and serve with boiled potatoes and Red Cabbage (see recipe).

1 leg of venison (about 6 to 8 pounds)
½ cup Coleman's English mustard
½ cup brown sugar
2 cups Madeira or port
2 tablespoons Cognac or brandy
2 sprigs thyme

Preheat the oven to 325°F.

Rub the venison with mustard, then sprinkle with brown sugar. Wrap in foil, pouring on Madeira or port, Cognac, and thyme sprigs before closing the foil tightly. Bake 2 hours, or until a meat thermometer registers 175°F. for medium, 185°F. for well-done. Raise the oven temperature to 400°F., open the foil, and roast 10 minutes more to brown.

Pass any accumulated juices around as a sauce.

Venison Stew

SERVES 4 TO 6

1/2 pound salt pork
6 tablespoons butter, melted
2 tablespoons vegetable oil
3 pounds lean venison meat, trimmed of fat and nerves, cut into 2-inch
    cubes
1 1/3 cups diced onions
1 cup diced celery
2 cups dry red wine
Salt and freshly ground pepper to taste
1/4 teaspoon dried thyme
1/4 teaspoon dried rosemary
2 cups small whole mushrooms, cleaned and trimmed
2 cups sour cream

Trim the rind from the salt pork, rinse in cold water, and par-
boil. Rinse the cooked pork, then cut into 1/2-inch dice. Fry the
pork over medium heat until crispy, then drain and discard the
fat, and set the pork aside.

Heat the butter and oil in a large skillet and brown the
venison cubes over high heat for 3 minutes, or until browned on
all sides. Remove the meat and set aside. Add the onions and
celery to the skillet and cook, stirring occasionally, until the
onions are golden brown.

Place the onions and celery in a stewpot, add the browned
meat, wine, and the seasonings and herbs. Bring to a boil, reduce heat, and simmer gently 20 minutes, or until the meat is
almost tender. Add the reserved salt pork, and stir in the mushrooms. Blend well, taste and adjust the seasoning, and simmer
gently another 20 minutes, or until fork-tender. Remove from
the heat and stir in the sour cream. Simmer over low heat for
10 minutes, but *do not boil.* Taste and adjust the seasoning. Serve
with buttered noodles or rice.

Marinade for Wild Game

MAKES ENOUGH FOR 8 TO 10 POUNDS OF MEAT

This marinade works well with venison, wild boar, rabbit, pheasant, alligator, raccoon, buffalo—all wild game. Any leftover marinade can be strained, boiled, and frozen for use another time. Vegetables from the marinade can be added to your meat dish and cooked, if you wish.

1 quart dry red wine
1 ½ cups red wine vinegar
1 cup good-quality olive oil
2 onions, sliced
2 celery stalks, chopped
6 sprigs thyme
4 shallots, crushed
4 garlic cloves, crushed
2 carrots, finely sliced
6 whole cloves
12 peppercorns
10 juniper berries
1 pinch of salt
1 bay leaf

Blend all the ingredients together, and marinate the meat in the mixture for 24 to 48 hours, covered, in the refrigerator. The smaller the animal you are marinating, the less time it will need to be tenderized. Wild boar, venison, and alligator should be marinated 48 hours; for rabbits, raccoons, and wild birds, 24 hours should be sufficient.

Braised Buffalo or Beef Tongue with Wine-Mushroom Sauce

SERVES 8

This is an occasional special in Dominique's. Try it with beef tongue if buffalo tongue is not available. It's simple to prepare and very delicious.

1 fresh buffalo tongue (approximately 4 pounds) or beef tongue
2 tablespoons olive oil
2 small onions, peeled
2 garlic cloves, crushed
Juice of 1 lemon
1 small bay leaf
1 teaspoon salt
1 teaspoon peppercorns
1/4 cup soy sauce
4 tablespoons butter
1 pound mushrooms, cleaned, trimmed, and thickly sliced
3 tablespoons all-purpose flour, or 2 tablespoons cornstarch
3/4 cup dry white wine
1 tablespoon Worcestershire sauce
Lemon wedges for garnish (optional)

Put the tongue in a large kettle and cover with cold water. Bring to a boil and simmer, covered, 2 hours. Remove the tongue and cut away the fat, bones, and gristle with a small sharp knife. Measure out 6 cups cooking liquid, and set aside.

Clean and dry the kettle. Add the oil and heat over medium heat. Add the tongue and brown on all sides, being careful not to pierce the meat when turning (use tongs). Add the reserved cooking liquid, onions, garlic, lemon juice, bay leaf, salt, and peppercorns. Bring to a boil, reduce heat, and simmer 30 minutes. Pierce the tongue with a two-pronged fork in 5 or 6 places. Add soy sauce and stir to combine. Continue simmering the tongue 1 hour more, covered.

Remove the tongue to a heated platter and keep warm. Strain the liquid in the kettle, discarding the solids. Melt the butter in a skillet and sauté the mushrooms for 4 minutes. Stir in the flour or cornstarch and cook, stirring, about 3 minutes. Add the wine, Worcestershire, and 1 ½ cups strained cooking liquid. Boil gently until the sauce thickens.

Carve the tongue diagonally in ¼-inch-thick slices, starting at the tip. Arrange the slices on a platter, and pour the sauce over the meat. Serve warm with lemon wedges, if desired.

Breast of Wild Duck Bourguignon

SERVES 4

Winter weather makes this warming dish a star at Dominique's in Washington, D.C.

8 raw duck breasts, skinned
4 tablespoons butter
2 tablespoons vegetable or peanut oil
1 ½ cups dry red wine
Salt and freshly ground pepper to taste
1 cup sliced mushrooms
⅓ cup diced celery leaves
½ cup Chicken Stock (see recipe)
1 bouquet garni (see p. 32)
⅓ cup light cream
2 tablespoons Armagnac
Red Cabbage (see recipe)
Juice of 1 lemon

Rinse the duck breasts under cold water and pat dry with paper towels. Heat the butter and oil in a large skillet over medium-high heat. When the fat begins to sizzle, add the breast meat and cook 3 minutes on each side, or until golden brown. Remove all but 2 tablespoons of fat from the pan and lower the heat to medium, leaving the duck in the skillet. Add ½ cup wine, salt and pepper, the mushrooms, and celery leaves. Simmer 4 to 5 minutes, then add remaining 1 cup wine and the chicken stock and bring to a boil. Add the bouquet garni. Reduce heat and simmer 15 minutes.

Remove the duck breasts to a warm platter. Simmer the sauce to reduce to 1 ½ cups. While the sauce is reducing, slice the duck breasts thinly and keep warm. Remove the bouquet garni from the reduced sauce and discard. Strain the sauce through a fine sieve, pressing down on the vegetables with the back of a wooden spoon to extract their flavor. Transfer the sauce to a saucepan, add the cream, and season to taste. Stir in the Armagnac, bring to a boil, and cook 1 minute.

Place the prepared cabbage on a serving platter, top with duck slices, and squeeze lemon juice over the meat. Serve with the sauce on the side.

Canada Goose in the Bag

SERVES 4

Hunters often hesitate to spend the time searching for wild goose because often, when cooked, it can become tough and tasteless. But, starting well in advance to marinate the bird, this recipe is guaranteed to result in a tender meal, unless the goose is one hundred years old!

1 wild goose, cleaned (5 to 8 pounds)
1 bottle plus 1 cup dry red wine
⅓ cup red wine vinegar
2 sprigs thyme, or 1 teaspoon dried
½ cup butter
Salt and freshly ground pepper to taste
1 large onion, coarsely chopped
6 celery stalks, coarsely chopped
16 small white mushrooms, cleaned and trimmed
1½ teaspoons cornstarch, dissolved in ½ cup fresh orange juice

Marinate the goose in a full bottle of wine, the vinegar, and thyme for 48 hours, covered, in the refrigerator, turning from time to time. Remove the goose and pat dry, discarding the marinade.

Preheat the oven to 375°F.

Place the goose, butter, salt, pepper, onion, celery, mushrooms, 1 cup wine, and dissolved cornstarch in a special roasting bag. Secure the bag and shake gently to blend all the ingredients. Make a slit in the top of the bag, then roast about 1 hour, until done. Strain the accumulated liquid and use for gravy.

Wild Goose, Hunter Style

SERVES 4 TO 6

Hunters get up at 5:00 A.M. or earlier, so by the time they get back to the lodge at night, they want something simple and easy to cook—uncomplicated but delicious. Wild Goose, Hunter Style, is just the thing!

1 *wild goose, cleaned*
2 *onions, quartered*
2 *apples, cored and quartered*
6 *strips of bacon*
1 *carrot, sliced*
1 *bay leaf*
1 *pinch of dried thyme*
1 *onion, diced*
1 *celery stalk with leaves, sliced*
3 *sprigs parsley, chopped*
3 ¾ *cups Chicken Stock (see recipe)*
2 *tablespoons cornstarch, dissolved in* ¼ *cup water*

Preheat the oven to 450°F.

Stuff the goose with quartered onions and the apples. Cover with bacon strips and brown in the preheated oven 15 minutes. Remove the fat from the roasting pan and discard. Add the carrot, bay leaf, thyme, diced onion, celery, parsley, and stock, and cover tightly with foil. Reduce the heat to 375°F. and roast 2½ hours, basting often.

Remove the goose to a heated platter. Strain the pan juices and thicken, over medium heat, with the dissolved cornstarch. The choicest part of the goose is the breast, so eat that yourself, and serve your guests the legs!

Wild Goose
in a Mustard-Crumb Crust

SERVES 4 TO 6

This recipe can be made by substituting 4 breasts of wild goose for the whole goose; in such instances, reduce the roasting time to 35 minutes before applying the mustard-crumb crust.

1 wild goose, cleaned (6 to 8 pounds)
1 bottle dry white wine
6 celery stalks, cut into 2-inch pieces
2 large onions, quartered
6 garlic cloves, crushed
2 carrots, cut into large chunks
Salt and freshly ground pepper to taste
6 1/2 ounces Dijon mustard
2 cups fresh or packaged herbed bread crumbs

Place the goose in a deep stovetop casserole or Dutch oven. Add the wine and enough water to cover the bird completely. Add the celery, onions, garlic, carrots, salt, and pepper. Bring to a boil, reduce heat, and simmer until tender, about 30 to 40 minutes, skimming from time to time.

Preheat the oven to 350°F.

Remove the goose to a roasting pan. Strain the broth, reserving the vegetables and 1 cup strained liquid. Add the vegetables and 1/2 cup broth to the roasting pan and cook 1 hour, basting the goose often with the remaining 1/2 cup reserved broth. Remove the bird and set aside to cool. Discard the remaining ingredients in the roasting pan.

When cooled, brush the entire bird with mustard. Cover with the bread crumbs, pressing into the mustard to be sure they adhere. Return the goose to the oven and roast 15 minutes more, or until the crust is browned. Serve hot or cold.

Oven-Barbecued Alligator

SERVES 4

We serve this in both our restaurants, to much applause. Remember, insist on steaks cut from the center section of the tail. Serve with Creamy Coleslaw and Hush Puppies (see recipes).

Four 12-ounce alligator steaks (about ½ inch thick), from center cut of
*   tail (see p. 185)*
⅔ cup lemon juice
½ cup soy sauce
2 tablespoons chopped parsley
1½ cups vegetable oil
4 drops of Tabasco sauce
Salt and freshly ground pepper to taste
4 garlic cloves, minced
About 1 cup bread crumbs

GARLIC BUTTER

4 tablespoons unsalted butter, at room temperature
2 tablespoons finely chopped parsley
1 garlic clove, minced
1 pinch of salt

Remove all the fat and connective tissue from the meat. Pound each steak between sheets of wax paper until ¼ inch thick, using a wooden mallet (as for veal scallopini). In a shallow pan or bowl, combine the lemon juice, soy sauce, parsley, oil, Tabasco, salt, pepper, and garlic. Add the alligator steaks, cover, and refrigerate 8 hours, turning the meat occasionally.

Preheat the oven to 375°F.

Remove the steaks from the marinade and drain, then sprinkle with salt and pepper. Dip the steaks in the bread crumbs, shaking off the excess. Arrange in a shallow pan.

To make the garlic butter, blend all the ingredients well. Top each steak with one-quarter of the garlic butter, and bake about 25 minutes, or until the meat is tender.

Creole-Style Alligator

SERVES 4 TO 6

The alligator must marinate for 2 days before cooking.

2 pounds alligator meat, from center cut of tail (see p. 185)
Marinade for Wild Game (see recipe)
1/4 cup butter
1 large red pepper, seeded and diced
3/4 cup chopped onion
1 cup chopped celery with leaves
1/4 cup sifted all-purpose flour
One 20-ounce can tomatoes, with juice
8 fresh tomatoes, peeled, seeded, and finely chopped
Salt and freshly ground pepper to taste
1 tablespoon brown sugar
2 bay leaves
4 whole cloves
3 tablespoons Worcestershire sauce
1/8 teaspoon Tabasco sauce (optional)
1 tablespoon lemon juice
1/3 cup dry white wine

Remove all the fat and connective tissue from the meat, and cut into 2-inch cubes. Then marinate in a glass bowl, covered and refrigerated, for 48 hours in Marinade for Wild Game.

In a large skillet, melt the butter. Sauté the red pepper, onion, and celery for 10 minutes, or until the vegetables are tender. Sprinkle flour over the vegetables and cook, stirring, for 3 minutes. Remove from the heat and stir in the canned and fresh tomatoes. Add salt and pepper, brown sugar, bay leaves, and cloves, and return the pan to the heat. Bring to a boil, stirring constantly.

Drain the alligator meat, add to pan, and return the mixture to a boil. Reduce the heat and simmer, uncovered, 45 minutes, stirring occasionally. Remove from the heat, remove and discard the bay leaf, stir in the Worcestershire, Tabasco if desired, lemon juice, and wine. Taste and adjust the seasoning. Serve over hot rice.

Fried Alligator Tail

SERVES 4

This is a simplified, home version of one of our guests' favorite Miami Beach recipes. I learned this recipe originally while duck hunting. The alligators were eating the ducks and upsetting our hunt, so we decided to do something about it! This recipe, using cornmeal, was the specialty of the Mexican man with whom I was hunting. It, too, must be begun well in advance.

2 pounds alligator meat, from center cut of tail (see p. 185)
Salt and freshly ground pepper to taste
Marinade for Wild Game (see recipe)
2 cups yellow cornmeal
Oil for frying
2 tablespoons chopped fresh parsley for garnish

Remove all the fat and connective tissue from the meat, then cut into 2-inch cubes. Combine the meat with the marinade in a glass bowl, cover, and refrigerate 48 hours, stirring occasionally with a wooden spoon.

Remove the meat from the marinade and pat dry on paper towels. Place the cornmeal in a paper bag, then add the cubes, a few at a time, and shake to coat. Fry the coated cubes in hot oil (375°F.) until golden brown. Dust with chopped parsley, and serve hot with a spicy tartar or cocktail sauce.

Sautéed Florida Alligator "Paws"

SERVES 4

1 pound Florida alligator meat, from center cut of tail fillet or jowl meat
   (see p. 185)
1 cup all-purpose flour, seasoned with salt and pepper
2 large eggs, lightly beaten
½ cup Clarified Butter (see recipe)
Lemon wedges for garnish
Parsley for garnish

Remove all the fat and connective tissue from the meat. Slice
into medaillions about ½ inch thick, and pound, as you would
veal, until very thin. Dredge the meat in the seasoned flour,
shaking off the excess. Dip each piece in beaten egg, allowing
the excess to drip off. Then quickly sauté the meat in clarified
butter until golden brown on both sides. Drain on paper towels.
Garnish with lemon wedges and parsley, and serve with mustard
on the side.

Desserts
and
Breads

The remembrance of any meal is greatly affected by the lingering impression left by dessert. I was only a teenager in Lyons when I first went to work in a pastry shop. At age twenty, I was head pastry chef at Père Bise in Talloires, then on to Paris, Brown's Hotel in London, the Americana in Bal Harbour, Florida, the Shoreham in Washington. So, therefore, this final chapter of dessert and bread recipes is close to my heart. I have written two pastry and dessert cookbooks already, *The Modern Pastry Chef's Guide to Professional Baking* in 1962, and *The Chef's Dessert Cookbook* in 1975. Each book contained hundreds of wonderful recipes. To select just a few for this chapter, well, it was not an easy task! I tried to include recipes that are very special. There are classics from Dominique's restaurants, such as Key Lime Pie and Elizabeth Taylor's Chocolate Truffles. And some specialties from our chef in Miami Beach, including Strawberry Mille-feuille with Hot Caramel Sauce, and one dessert so popular that we now serve it in Washington, D.C., too—Cheese Mousse with Raspberry Sauce. And, finally, you'll find a few of my personal favorites, such as Clafouti, the cherry torte served in the French countryside, and the Pain d'Épice we include in the Dominique's bread baskets at Thanksgiving. So read on, my friend, and *bon appétit.*

Pastry Cream

MAKES 1 1/4 CUPS

Besides being a classic filling for cream puffs and éclairs, pastry cream is commonly used on the bottom of fruit tarts, between cake layers, and, thickened, in some soufflés.

3 egg yolks
1/3 cup sugar less 2 tablespoons
2 tablespoons cornstarch
2 tablespoons all-purpose flour
1 cup milk, scalded
1 vanilla bean, or 1 teaspoon vanilla extract

Place the yolks in an electric mixer and gradually beat in the sugar. Beat 3 minutes to combine well. Sift together the cornstarch and flour, and add to the egg mixture. Add the milk in a slow stream, beating until incorporated. Transfer the mixture to a heavy saucepan and bring to a boil, stirring constantly with a wire whisk. Simmer about 3 minutes, or until thick. Add the vanilla, then transfer the pastry cream to a glass bowl, cover the surface with a lightly buttered round of wax paper, and remove the vanilla bean once cooled to room temperature. Set aside (or refrigerate) until ready to use.

Crème Fraîche

MAKES 1 CUP

This is sometimes difficult to purchase in America, so we make our own crème fraîche at Dominique's. It is used in many desserts, and can replace whipped cream with fresh-fruit desserts.

1 cup heavy cream
1 1/2 teaspoons buttermilk

Blend the cream and buttermilk in a glass jar, cover, and set in a warm place for 8 to 10 hours, or until thickened. Refrigerate until ready to use. It keeps for about 5 days in the refrigerator.

Sauce Liqueur

MAKES 1 1/2 CUPS

Any liqueur of your choice may be used in this recipe. It is wonderful served with soufflés, so experiment with it and any of the soufflés later in this chapter.

1/2 cup light cream
1/2 cup milk
3 egg yolks
3 tablespoons sugar
2 tablespoons liqueur of your choice, such as curaçao, brandy, rum, Grand Marnier, and Chartreuse

Scald the cream and milk together in a heavy saucepan, and set aside. Beat the egg yolks and sugar with a fork or wire whisk until light, then beat in the hot milk and cream in a slow stream until fully incorporated. Transfer the sauce to the top of a double boiler and heat over hot water, beating constantly, until the sauce thickens and coats the back of a spoon. *Do not boil.* Remove from the heat and let cool. Stir in the liqueur.

Sabayon Sauce

SERVES 4

Serve this over any fresh-fruit dessert, with our Don Johnson Pistachio Soufflé or Iced Key Lime Soufflé (see recipes).

4 egg yolks
3 tablespoons sugar
1/4 teaspoon vanilla
1/2 cup rum

In the top of a double boiler over hot water, beat the egg yolks and sugar together for about 10 minutes, or until ribbons are formed when the beater is lifted and the mixture is quite thick. Add the vanilla and rum very gradually, beating constantly, until all is well incorporated.

Apple Tart

MAKES TWO 8-INCH TARTS

Our guests in Miami Beach keep the kitchen busy preparing these delicious tarts.

1 1/3 cups unbleached flour
1 teaspoon salt
1/2 cup unsalted butter, chilled
1/4 cup ice water, or as needed
3 to 4 firm cooking apples, such as Granny Smith or Golden Delicious
Juice of 1/2 lemon
2 tablespoons sugar
3/4 cup Pastry Cream (see recipe)
Apricot jam, melted and strained

Place the flour and salt in a bowl and cut in the chilled butter with a pastry blender, until the mixture resembles coarse meal. Sprinkle on the ice water and stir quickly with a fork, until the mixture holds together, adding a few more drops if necessary. Gather the pastry into a ball, flatten, and wrap tightly in plastic wrap. Chill in the refrigerator for at least 1 hour.

Preheat the oven to 400°F.

Peel, core, and halve the apples. Slice thinly into a bowl, sprinkling with lemon juice to keep the slices from darkening. Stir in the sugar and set aside.

Divide the pastry in half, and roll out in 2 circles to fit 8-inch tart pans with removable bottoms. Line the pans with the pastry, and trim the edges. Spread half the pastry cream in each tart shell, then arrange the apple slices in circles on top, overlapping slightly. Bake until the pastry is evenly browned. Remove from the oven to racks to cool, brushing the apple slices with apricot jam while still hot to give the tarts a good glaze. Serve warm or cold.

Clafouti

MAKES ONE 9-INCH TORTE

This cherry torte is a traditional cake from the French country-side, where children love it! It is a simple but very savory dessert.

²/₃ cup sifted all-purpose flour
1 ¹/₃ cups milk
¹/₃ cup granulated sugar
3 eggs, lightly beaten
1 teaspoon vanilla extract
1 teaspoon kirsch (optional)
1 pinch of salt
3 cups pitted fresh black cherries, or drained and pitted canned Bing
    cherries
Confectioners' sugar

Preheat the oven to 350°F.

Grease a 9-inch baking dish or pie tin and set aside. Place the flour in a deep bowl and gradually stir in the milk. Add the granulated sugar and eggs and beat until all the lumps are dissolved. Stir in the vanilla, kirsch if desired, and salt, combining well. Pour half the batter into the prepared baking dish or pie tin. Distribute the cherries over the batter, then top with the remaining batter. Bake 50 minutes, or until a knife inserted in the center comes out clean. Dust with confectioners' sugar, and serve warm.

Key Lime Pie

MAKES ONE 9-INCH PIE

If you can't find fresh Key limes in your area, you can probably find bottled Key lime juice.

3 eggs, separated
One 14-ounce can sweetened condensed milk
¾ cup freshly squeezed Key lime juice, rinds grated and reserved
1 Prebaked Pie Shell (see following recipe)
1 teaspoon sugar

Beat the egg yolks together in a mixing bowl. Beat in the condensed milk and lime juice, and pour the mixture into the prebaked pie shell. Refrigerate about 2 hours, or until set.

Preheat the oven to 375°F.

Beat the egg whites until stiff but not dry. Fold in the reserved grated lime rind (if using bottled juice, skip this). Spread the meringue on top of the chilled pie in decorative swirls, being sure to cover to the outer edge of crust all around. Dust with sugar, then bake 7 or 8 minutes, until the meringue topping is lightly browned. Cool before serving, but *do not refrigerate.*

Prebaked Pie Shell

MAKES ONE 9-INCH PIE SHELL

1 cup sifted all-purpose flour
³⁄₈ teaspoon salt
¹⁄₂ teaspoon superfine sugar
¹⁄₃ cup shortening (half butter, half vegetable shortening), at room temperature
2 to 3 tablespoons ice water

Chill the flour in the refrigerator for 5 minutes. Sift the flour, salt, and sugar together into a mixing bowl. Blend the shortenings to combine, then cut them into the flour mixture with a pastry blender, until it resembles coarse meal. Sprinkle ice water over all, 1 tablespoon at a time, and toss with your fingertips or a fork until dough just holds together. Form into a ball, flatten, wrap tightly in plastic wrap, and refrigerate for at least 2 hours or overnight.

To prepare the crust, set out the pastry at room temperature for a few minutes, then roll out on a lightly floured board to ⅛ inch thickness. Fold the dough in half, lift gently into a 9-inch pie tin, and then unfold. Trim the overhanging edges, and refrigerate the crust to chill thoroughly.

Preheat the oven to 425°F.

Remove the pie crust from the refrigerator and prick all over with the tines of a fork. Cover the dough with a 14-inch-round of wax paper, and fill with dried beans or uncooked rice (or use pie weights, if available). Bake 15 minutes. Remove the pie tin from the oven and reduce the heat to 400°F. Remove the beans, rice, or weights and wax paper, then return the shell to the oven and bake 15 minutes more, or until golden brown. The pie shell must be cooked thoroughly and cooled completely before filling.

Flourless Chocolate Cake

SERVES 6 TO 8

I guarantee this cake will be a hit, wherever you serve it!

20 ounces imported semisweet chocolate
2 ½ sticks (10 ounces) unsalted butter
10 egg yolks
1 tablespoon sifted cornstarch
⅓ cup espresso or double-strength coffee, cooled to room temperature
1 cup cold milk
5 egg whites

FOR COATING

4 ounces imported semisweet chocolate
1 tablespoon unsalted butter
1 tablespoon heavy cream

Preheat the oven to 300°F.

Melt 20 ounces semisweet chocolate with 2 ½ sticks butter in the top of a double boiler. In a mixing bowl with an electric mixer or hand-held beater, beat the egg yolks. Gradually add the cornstarch, coffee, and milk. Blend the melted chocolate and butter into the egg mixture and stir to combine well.

In a separate bowl, beat the egg whites until stiff but not dry. Gently fold into the chocolate mixture, then transfer to a buttered and floured 10-inch cake pan. Bake in a hot-water bath for 1 ½ hours. Remove the cake pan to a rack and let cool. Place the cooled cake in the refrigerator, covered, for at least 3 hours before serving.

Before serving time, prepare the coating. Melt all the coating ingredients in the top of a double boiler. Remove from the heat and set in refrigerator to cool for a few minutes. Spread coating over cake, and refrigerate until coating hardens.

Lime Pound Cake

SERVES 6 TO 8

This is one of my personal recipes, delicious any time of day as a snack or dessert.

2 cups sifted all-purpose flour
1/4 teaspoon baking soda
2 1/4 cups granulated sugar
1 1/2 cups lightly salted butter, at room temperature
2 tablespoons lime juice
1 tablespoon vanilla extract
1 teaspoon grated lime rind
1 teaspoon grated orange rind
7 eggs, separated
1/2 teaspoon cream of tartar
Confectioners' sugar

Preheat the oven to 325°F.

Lightly grease and flour a 10-cup fluted tube pan or similar cake mold, and set aside. In a mixing bowl, sift together the flour, baking soda, and 1 1/4 cups granulated sugar. In a separate bowl, cream the butter. Stir the flour mixture into the butter just until combined. Do not overmix. Add the lime juice, vanilla, and lime and orange rinds and stir to combine. Add the egg yolks, 1 at a time, beating well after each addition.

In a separate bowl, beat the egg whites and cream of tartar until stiff but not dry, gradually adding remaining 1 cup granulated sugar. Gently fold the egg whites into the batter, then pour into the prepared pan and bake 1 hour and 15 minutes, or until the cake tests done. Let cake cool in the pan on a rack for 20 minutes, then invert the cake on the rack, dust with confectioners' sugar, and let cool completely before serving.

Pears Andalousie

SERVES 4

4 whole Bartlett pears
1 1/2 cups currant jelly
2 cups water
2 egg yolks
1/4 cup plus 1 teaspoon sugar
1 teaspoon kirsch
1/3 cup heavy cream

Peel the pears, leaving the stems intact. Combine the jelly and water in a saucepan large enough to accommodate the fruit and bring to a boil. Add the pears to the hot syrup, cover, and simmer until the pears are tender, about 10 to 15 minutes. Remove the saucepan from the heat, let cool, then refrigerate.

To prepare the sauce, combine the egg yolks and 1/4 cup sugar in a deep bowl or in the top of a double boiler. Place over hot water and beat until thick. Stir in the kirsch and continue beating for 1 minute. Remove from the heat and set the bowl in a pan filled with ice cubes, stirring to chill.

At serving time, beat the cream with 1 teaspoon sugar until stiff, then fold into the chilled egg yolk mixture. Remove the pears from the syrup and arrange on a serving tray or platter. Discard the syrup. Coat the pears with sauce, and serve at once.

Strawberry Mille-feuille
with Hot Caramel Sauce

SERVES 4

This Miami Beach special is so good and popular that we now serve it in Washington, D.C., as well.

Pastry Dough (see following recipe)
⅔ cup heavy cream
4 teaspoons granulated sugar
2½ cups Pastry Cream (see recipe), at room temperature
1 pound strawberries, rinsed, hulled, and sliced
4 tablespoons confectioners' sugar for garnish
2 strawberries, halved, for garnish

HOT CARAMEL SAUCE

1 cup granulated sugar
⅓ cup water
1½ cups heavy cream

Prepare the pastry dough, being sure to cook fully and let cool.

Whip ⅔ cup heavy cream with 4 teaspoons granulated sugar until the cream is stiff and holds peaks. Fold into the prepared pastry cream and set aside.

Place 1 piece of baked pastry dough on a platter, cover with half the pastry cream mixture, then top with half the sliced strawberries. Place a second piece of pastry on top, and cover with the remaining pastry cream mixture. Top with the remaining sliced strawberries and a third piece of pastry, smooth side down. Dust the top with confectioners' sugar, and decorate with strawberry halves.

To prepare the caramel sauce, combine 1 cup granulated sugar and water in a 1½-quart saucepan and heat over medium-high heat, stirring constantly, until the sugar turns a caramel color, being careful not to let it burn. Remove from the heat and gradually stir in 1½ cups heavy cream. Return to the stove and bring the sauce to a boil, stirring, then remove from the heat.

To serve, cut the assembled mille-feuille into 4 portions with a serrated knife. Pour the hot caramel sauce onto 4 dessert plates and top with a portion of mille-feuille. This dessert does not keep; it must be served at once.

Pastry Dough for Strawberry Mille-feuille

MAKES 1 POUND PASTRY DOUGH, COOKED IN 3 PIECES

It is important to use good-quality all-purpose flour, and to brush off any accumulated flour from the dough after each folding. Be sure to follow the instructions carefully; each step is important. The pastry dough may be prepared several days in advance and baked when ready to use.

½ pound unsalted butter, chilled
½ pound all-purpose flour
½ teaspoon salt
About ¾ cup ice water

Knead the butter with your hands on a pastry board to remove the water. Squeeze it firmly and work it to a pliable, smooth consistency. Form the butter into a ½-inch-thick square, and chill it in the refrigerator.

Sift the flour and salt together in a deep bowl; make a well in the center and pour in the water, beating constantly. Add only enough ice water to obtain a dough of about the same consistency as the butter; remember, the dough will soften slightly while it rests. Cover the dough with a damp towel and let it rest in the refrigerator for 30 minutes.

Roll out the dough on a lightly floured board in a square about ¾ inch thick. Place the butter in the center of the square, fold the 4 sides of the dough over the butter, and press firmly with your hands to secure the butter inside the dough. Roll out to a rectangle three times longer than it is wide. Work gently to ensure that the dough doesn't tear. Fold the rectangle in thirds, top to middle and bottom to middle. You will have a square the same size as your original shape. This rolling and folding is called a turn. Let the dough rest in a cool place (not the refrigerator) for 30 minutes. After the first turn, too much cold will prevent the butter from mixing properly.

Repeat the rolling and folding for a second turn, then chill the dough in refrigerator for 20 minutes. Repeat for a total of six turns in all. Chill for 1 hour after the final turn. Pastry can be made up to this point several days in advance, if stored flat on a lightly floured board, covered with a damp towel, in the refrigerator.

Preheat the oven to 425°F.

Roll out the pastry dough to a rectangle about ¹⁄₁₆ inch thick. Cut it with a very sharp knife into 3 pieces, about 6 inches by 8 inches each. Place the dough on a baking sheet and prick all over with the tines of a fork. Bake 25 minutes, or until golden. Do not open the oven door to check until the rising is completed. Remove the cooked pastry to a rack and let it cool thoroughly.

Cheese Mousse
with Raspberry Sauce

SERVES 4

This excellent dessert is served in Washington, D.C., and Miami Beach.

½ cup sugar
⅓ cup water
2 egg yolks
2 tablespoons raspberry liqueur
⅓ cup sour cream or softened cream cheese
2 envelopes unflavored gelatin
6 tablespoons cold water
½ cup heavy cream

RASPBERRY SAUCE

½ pint fresh raspberries
½ cup water
1 cup sugar
Fresh mint leaves for garnish

Place ½ cup sugar and ⅓ cup water in a heavy saucepan and bring to a boil over medium-high heat. Stir until the sugar dissolves, then boil undisturbed for 5 minutes. Remove from the heat and set aside.

In a mixing bowl, beat the egg yolks well. Slowly add the reserved syrup and continue beating for 10 minutes to make a thick and creamy mixture. Add the raspberry liqueur and sour cream or cream cheese and mix well.

In a small saucepan, soften the gelatin in 6 tablespoons cold water, then dissolve over low heat. Add the gelatin to the egg mixture and stir to combine.

In another bowl, beat the heavy cream until very stiff, and fold into the egg mixture. The mousse should have a very smooth texture. Pour the mousse into 4 individual lightly oiled soufflé molds and chill in the refrigerator for at least 2 hours.

Pick over the raspberries and set 4 aside for garnish. Combine ½ cup water with 1 cup sugar in a small saucepan and boil until the sugar dissolves. Set aside to cool. In the work bowl of a food processor fitted with a steel blade, or in a blender, combine the cooled syrup and raspberries and process to a fine purée. Strain the sauce to remove the seeds.

To serve, spoon some sauce onto each of 4 dessert plates. Dip the soufflé molds into a bowl of hot water for a few seconds, then turn out onto the dessert plates. Top with the remaining sauce, and garnish with the reserved raspberries and fresh mint leaves.

NOTE: If fresh raspberries are not available, fresh strawberries may be substituted.

Lime Mousse

SERVES 4

4 limes
1/3 cup water
1/2 cup sugar
2 envelopes unflavored gelatin
4 tablespoons cold water
1 1/2 cups heavy cream, whipped stiff

Chill 4 champagne glasses or wine goblets in the freezer for 1 hour.

Grate the zest (green part) of the limes and set aside. Remove the white pith, membranes, and seeds and discard. You should have 1 cup pulp. Reserve.

Place 1/3 cup water and the sugar in a small saucepan and bring to a boil. Stir until the sugar dissolves, then continue to boil undisturbed for 3 minutes. Remove from the heat and set aside.

In a small saucepan, soften the gelatin in 4 tablespoons cold water, then dissolve over low heat.

Combine the lime pulp, grated zest, and sugar syrup. Stir in the dissolved gelatin and mix well. Fold in the whipped cream. Pour the mousse into the chilled goblets and freeze for 1 hour before serving.

White Chocolate Mousse

SERVES 4

We serve this in both restaurants, garnished with Chocolate Leaves (see recipe).

9 1/2 ounces white chocolate, broken into small pieces
3 egg yolks
1 cup heavy cream
3 tablespoons Amaretto
1 tablespoon vanilla extract
6 egg whites
1 pinch of salt
2 tablespoons sugar

Melt the chocolate in the top of a double boiler, or place it in a very low (180°F.) oven for about 10 minutes. Set aside.

Whisk the egg yolks until pale yellow and thick, then add cream and combine well. Heat the mixture in the top of a double boiler or in a heavy saucepan over low heat, beating constantly, until the custard thickens and coats the back of a spoon. *Do not boil.* Transfer the custard to a large bowl and add the Amaretto, vanilla, and reserved chocolate, stirring well to combine. Place the mixture in the refrigerator to cool.

In a separate bowl, beat the egg whites and salt until frothy, then continue beating until stiff peaks form, gradually adding the sugar. Stir one-fourth of the beaten egg whites into the cooled mousse mixture, then gently fold in the remaining whites. Refrigerate until well chilled. Serve cold, garnished with Chocolate Leaves, whipped cream, or berries, if you wish.

Mocha Pots de Crème

SERVES 6

2 cups light cream
1 1/2 tablespoons instant coffee
6 egg yolks
1/2 cup sugar
1 pinch of salt

Preheat the oven to 325°F.

Scald the cream, then remove from the heat and stir in the coffee until dissolved.

In a deep bowl, beat the egg yolks, sugar, and salt until light and fluffy. Gradually add the cream mixture, beating constantly.

Strain the mixture, then pour into 6 individual custard cups or ramekins. Cover tightly with foil, place in a roasting pan, and fill the pan with hot water to halfway up the sides of the cups. Bake 15 to 18 minutes, or until the point of a knife inserted into the center comes out clean. Chill before serving.

Vanilla Crème Brûlée

SERVES 4

2 cups heavy cream
1 vanilla bean, or 1/2 teaspoon vanilla extract
1 pinch of salt
5 egg yolks
1/3 cup plus 2 tablespoons granulated sugar
3 tablespoons light brown sugar, blended with 2 tablespoons granulated
    sugar, for topping

Preheat the oven to 300°F.

In a heavy saucepan, combine the cream, vanilla, and salt and bring to a simmer over medium heat. In a large bowl, beat the egg yolks and granulated sugar with a wire whisk. Gradually add the hot cream, removing the vanilla bean and reserving for future use. Skim off any bubbles that form on top of custard.

Set four ¾-cup custard cups in a roasting pan, and fill the cups to the top with custard. Place the roasting pan in the oven and fill with enough hot water to reach halfway up the sides of the custard cups. Cover the pan loosely with foil and bake 1 hour, or until the custard is firm. Remove the custard cups from the hot-water bath and cool on a rack, then transfer to the refrigerator to chill for 1 hour, or until cold.

Preheat the broiler.

Sprinkle the blended light brown and granulated sugars evenly on top of the custards. Broil the custards quickly, until the sugar is caramelized, about 1 minute. Cool to room temperature, and serve.

Orange Crème Brûlée: Substitute the zest of 2 oranges for the vanilla, removing and discarding the zest after simmering it in the cream mixture.

Iced Key Lime Soufflé

SERVES 4 TO 6

If fresh Key limes are not available, substitute the limes you can find; the taste won't be authentic Key West, but you'll still have a wonderful soufflé! We serve this in Miami Beach with Sabayon Sauce (see recipe).

6 jumbo or 7 extra-large eggs, separated
1 1/2 cups plus 2 tablespoons sugar
1 1/2 tablespoons (1 1/2 envelopes) unflavored gelatin
2/3 cup strained Key lime juice
Grated zest of 3 Key limes
1 1/2 cups milk
1 scant tablespoon cornstarch
1 pinch of salt
1/2 cup heavy cream
1 tablespoon Cointreau

In a large bowl, beat together the egg yolks and 1 cup plus 2 tablespoons sugar until light yellow in color and slightly thickened. Set aside.

Soften the gelatin in the lime juice, and reserve.

Combine the grated lime zest with the milk and cornstarch in a saucepan and heat, stirring constantly, but *do not boil.* Pour the hot milk mixture into egg yolks in a thin stream, beating constantly. Transfer to the top of a double boiler over hot water and stir with a wooden spoon until the mixture thickens and coats the back of the spoon. Remove the custard from the heat, stir in the dissolved gelatin and lime juice, and set aside to cool to room temperature.

Beat the egg whites with a pinch of salt until soft peaks form. Add the remaining 1/2 cup sugar and continue beating until stiff. Fold the egg whites into the cooled lime-yolk mixture, and chill.

Whip the heavy cream with the Cointeau, and fold into the chilled custard.

Prepare a collar of oiled wax paper or foil to fit a 5- to 6-cup soufflé dish. Spoon the soufflé mixture into the dish, piling it to the top of the collar. Chill 3 or 4 hours in the refrigerator.

When ready to serve, run a sharp knife along the inside of the collar and gently remove it.

Don Johnson
Pistachio Soufflé

SERVES 4

From our Miami Beach menu, of course, this soufflé has been picked by Don Johnson as the best. We think of it as our "Miami Vice Special."

1 cup plus 1 tablespoon sugar
2 tablespoons water
4 ounces shelled pistachio nuts
2 egg yolks
⅓ cup sifted all-purpose flour
1 cup milk
1 tablespoon rum
4 egg whites
1 pinch of cream of tartar
Sabayon Sauce (see recipe)

In a heavy saucepan over medium heat, cook ½ cup sugar with 2 tablespoons water to the soft-ball stage, or until the sugar looks white and sandy. Add the pistachio nuts and continue cooking, stirring constantly, until the syrup turns a rich amber color. Pour out onto a buttered shallow baking pan to cool. When the pistachio brittle is cooled to room temperature, break it into small pieces and process it in a food processor fitted with a steel blade, until it is ground to a paste.

In an electric mixer, beat the egg yolks and ½ cup sugar until pale lemon-colored. Whisk in the flour and set aside.

In a large saucepan, bring the milk to a boil, add the pistachio-brittle paste, stir well, and boil 1 minute. Slowly pour the hot milk mixture into the egg yolks, stirring constantly. Return the milk-yolk mixture to the saucepan and bring to a boil over medium heat. Cook about 1 minute, stirring the bottom of the pan well with a wire whisk to prevent scorching, or until the mixture thickens. Transfer the mixture to a clean bowl, stir in the rum, and chill.

Preheat the oven to 450°F.

Butter 4 individual soufflé dishes, dust with the remaining tablespoon sugar, and set aside. Beat the egg whites with the cream of tartar until stiff but not dry. Gently fold the egg whites into the chilled pistachio cream, and scoop into the prepared soufflé dishes. Smooth the tops with a spatula, then run your thumb around the inside of each dish (this will form the "hat" of the soufflé). Bake 25 minutes.

While the soufflés are cooking, prepare the Sabayon Sauce. Serve the soufflés immediately from the oven, with the sauce on the side.

Fresh Raspberry Soufflé

SERVES 4 TO 6

The first time Ted Koppel came to Dominique's for dinner, he ordered this luscious dessert. We like to serve it with Sabayon Sauce, but you might want to follow in Mr. Koppel's footsteps and enjoy it with lots of fresh whipped cream.

2 tablespoons confectioners' sugar
1 1/2 cups very ripe fresh raspberries, cleaned
2 egg yolks, lightly beaten
1 pinch of cream of tartar
3/4 cup granulated sugar
7 egg whites
Sabayon Sauce (see recipe) or whipped cream for garnish

Preheat the oven to 375°F.

Butter a 1½-quart soufflé dish, and dust with confectioners' sugar. Set aside.

In a mixing bowl, crush about ¾ cup raspberries with the back of a spoon, then stir in the remaining whole berries. Add the egg yolks and stir to combine with the fruit.

In a separate bowl, beat the egg whites with cream of tartar until stiff but not dry, adding the granulated sugar gradually. Gently fold the egg whites into the berry mixture, and spoon into the prepared dish, smoothing the top with a spatula. Dust with the remaining confectioners' sugar, and bake 25 minutes, or until done.

While the soufflé is baking, prepare the Sabayon Sauce or whipped cream. Serve the soufflé immediately from oven, garnished with Sabayon Sauce or whipped cream.

Chocolate Leaves

MAKES 30 LEAVES

These are delicious on their own, and they also make a lovely garnish for any cold dessert, soufflé, or sorbet plate.

30 holly leaves
6 ounces semisweet chocolate

Wash and dry the holly leaves. Melt the chocolate over hot, not boiling, water. With a table knife or a brush, coat the backs of the leaves with the melted chocolate, making sure to leave a thick spine and not to spread the chocolate onto the front of the leaves. Place the leaves, chocolate side up, on a baking sheet lined with wax paper. Refrigerate until the chocolate is firm.

To remove the leaf from the chocolate, pull gently on the leaf stem; the chocolate and the leaf will separate.

Elizabeth Taylor's Chocolate Truffles

MAKES 42 TO 50 TRUFFLES

I created this recipe for a private birthday party we prepared for Miss Taylor, and we commemorate our good friend with this special dessert that we now serve at Dominique's in Washington, D.C.

1/2 cup heavy cream
3 tablespoons Grand Marnier
14 ounces Swiss or German sweet chocolate, broken into small pieces the size of a quarter
8 tablespoons unsalted butter, at room temperature
1 cup unsweetened cocoa, or as needed

Boil the cream in a small saucepan and reduce to 3 tablespoons. Remove from the heat and stir in the Grand Marnier and chocolate. Return the pan to very low heat and cook, stirring well, until the chocolate is melted. Whisk in the butter, 1 tablespoon at a time, and stir until all the ingredients are well combined and the texture is smooth and creamy. Place the chocolate mixture in the freezer for about 30 minutes.

With 2 cold teaspoons, scoop the chocolate into 1-inch balls. (For efficiency's sake, you may chill a few sets of teaspoons so, if one pair loses its chill, you'll have another pair ready.) Place each truffle in cocoa powder set in a bowl or small pan and roll to coat thoroughly.

Store the truffles in the refrigerator until ready to serve. Handle the truffles carefully; the heat of your hands will melt the delicate chocolate mixture.

French Country Beignets

MAKES ABOUT 36 BEIGNETS

We serve these in Washington, D.C., as a dessert, dusted liberally with confectioners' sugar. They make a nice addition to any brunch menu, too.

1 1/4 cups milk
1/3 cup plus 2 teaspoons granulated sugar
1 package (1/4 ounce) active dry yeast
About 3 1/2 cups all-purpose flour
2 eggs
2 tablespoons lard or vegetable shortening
1 teaspoon salt
1/2 teaspoon freshly grated nutmeg
Vegetable oil for frying
Confectioners' sugar for garnish

In a saucepan over low heat, combine the milk and 2 teaspoons sugar and heat to 110°F. Pour the warm milk into a glass bowl and stir in the yeast. Set aside for 5 to 10 minutes, or until foamy.

In the work bowl of a food processor fitted with a steel blade, or in a countertop mixer, combine 3 cups flour with the remaining 1/3 cup sugar, the eggs, lard or shortening, salt, and nutmeg and pulse 3 or 4 times to blend the ingredients. Add the yeast mixture and pulse 4 to 5 times to bring the dough together. The dough should be fairly smooth and nonsticky. If additional flour is needed, add the remaining flour, 1 or 2 tablespoons at a time, until the proper consistency is reached. Process 15 seconds to knead the dough, then turn out onto a lightly floured surface and form into a smooth ball. Lightly oil a large bowl, place the dough in the bowl, and turn to coat with oil on all sides. Cover the bowl with plastic wrap and let the dough rise in a warm, draft-free place until doubled in bulk, about 1 ½ hours.

Punch down the dough, turn out onto a lightly floured surface, and roll out to a rectangle about ½ inch thick. With a sharp knife, cut the dough into 2-inch strips on the diagonal, cross-hatching to form diamonds 2 inches wide. Carefully place the diamonds ½ inch apart on ungreased baking sheets. Cover loosely with plastic wrap. Gather any remaining dough scraps, knead together, let rest 15 minutes, then roll and cut as before. Repeat until all dough has been used. Let the covered beignets rise in a warm, draft-free place until almost doubled in bulk, about 45 minutes.

In a large saucepan or deep skillet, heat 3 inches of oil to 365°F., or until a 1-inch bread cube turns golden brown in 1 minute. Carefully slide the beignets into the oil, 3 or 4 at a time; do not crowd. Fry until puffy and golden brown on both sides, turning once with tongs. The cooking time is about 2 to 3 minutes per side. Drain on paper towels, sift confectioners' sugar over them, and serve hot.

Pain d'Épice

MAKES 2 LOAVES

This fine-textured French honey bread depends on long and vigorous beating—with an electric mixer set at medium speed for about 15 minutes, or with a wooden spoon or spatula for at least 20 minutes. We serve it at Dominique's in our bread baskets at Thanksgiving.

3 cups sifted all-purpose unbleached flour
1 cup rye flour
2 teaspoons salt
2 teaspoons baking powder
2 teaspoons baking soda
1/4 teaspoon powdered anise
1 teaspoon cinnamon
2 teaspoons ground ginger
1 cup shelled pistachio nuts or pecans (optional)
1 cup honey
2 eggs, lightly beaten
2 cups milk

Preheat the oven to 350°F.

Sift the dry ingredients together into a large mixing bowl. Stir in the honey, eggs, and milk, and beat until very light and smooth. Spoon the batter into 2 well-buttered 9-by-5-inch loaf pans, and bake 50 minutes, or until the breads test done.

Turn the loaves out onto a rack, cool completely, then wrap tightly in foil. Store the breads in the refrigerator for at least 3 days to allow the flavors to develop. Serve sliced thin, with unsalted butter.

Chive Biscuits

MAKES 12 BISCUITS

1 1/2 cups all-purpose flour, chilled in the freezer for 15 minutes
1 tablespoon baking powder
1/2 teaspoon salt
1 teaspoon sugar
3 tablespoons butter, chilled
1 tablespoon cold vegetable shortening
1/2 cup cold milk
1 egg yolk
4 tablespoons chopped fresh chives
2 tablespoons melted butter for glaze

Sift the dry ingredients together into a mixing bowl. With a pastry cutter or 2 knives, cut in the butter and shortening, until the mixture resembles coarse meal.

In a small bowl, combine the milk, egg yolk, and chives and stir to blend. Add the liquids to the shortening mixture and knead gently until all the ingredients are well blended. Place the dough in the refrigerator for at least 1 hour, or until just before serving time.

Preheat the oven to 425°F.

Roll out dough to ¾-inch thickness, and cut out biscuits with a 2-inch biscuit cutter. Grease and flour a cookie sheet. Place the biscuits on the cookie sheet and bake 8 to 10 minutes. Brush the tops with melted butter while still hot, and serve immediately.

Hush Puppies

SERVES 6

2 cups fine yellow cornmeal
2 teaspoons baking powder
1 teaspoon sugar
1 teaspoon salt
½ teaspoon freshly ground pepper
⅓ cup finely chopped onion
⅓ cup finely chopped green pepper
1 cup sour cream
⅓ cup canned creamed corn, drained
2 eggs
Oil for frying

In a mixing bowl, combine the cornmeal, baking powder, sugar, salt, and pepper. Add the onion and green pepper and stir to distribute evenly. Add the sour cream, corn, and eggs and beat well to combine.

Drop the batter by tablespoonfuls into oil heated to 375°F. Deep-fry until golden brown, turning often to brown evenly. Drain on paper towels, and serve hot with Oven-Barbecued Alligator (see recipe) or the fried fish of your choice.

Index

240